FIVE JEWISH LAWYERS
OF THE
COMMON LAW

FIVE JEWISH LAWYERS
OF THE
COMMON LAW

ARTHUR L. GOODHART

With a New Preface to This Edition
and a Supplement on
Mr. Justice Felix Frankfurter

Biography Index Reprint Series

BOOKS FOR LIBRARIES PRESS
FREEPORT, NEW YORK

INTERNATIONAL STANDARD BOOK NUMBER:
0-8369-8059-X

LIBRARY OF CONGRESS CATALOG CARD NUMBER:
79-148212

PRINTED IN THE UNITED STATES OF AMERICA

CONTENTS

PREFACE TO THE
    BOOKS FOR LIBRARIES EDITION   vii

FIVE JEWISH LAWYERS OF THE COMMON LAW   1

JUDAH PHILIP BENJAMIN   4

SIR GEORGE JESSEL   16

LOUIS D. BRANDEIS   24

RUFUS ISAACS, FIRST MARQUESS OF READING   39

BENJAMIN NATHAN CARDOZO   51

CONCLUSION   63

NOTES   67

SUPPLEMENT: MR. JUSTICE FRANKFURTER   75

THE Lucien Wolf Memorial Lecture has been instituted by the Jewish Historical Society of England in memory of Lucien Wolf (1857–1930), its founder and seven times its President. It is to be delivered annually by some person of eminence, Jewish or non-Jewish, and is to deal with any of the subjects with which Lucien Wolf's interests were particularly associated.

The eleventh lecture of the series, on *Five Jewish Lawyers of the Common Law*, was delivered on 15 May 1947, by Professor A. L. Goodhart, K.B.E., K.C., at University College, London University, with the Rt. Hon. Lord Chorley in the chair. The lecture, as printed here, has been considerably expanded.

PREFACE TO THE
BOOKS FOR LIBRARIES EDITION

When this lecture was delivered in 1947, I was careful to refer only to those distinguished jurists who were no longer living. I therefore made no reference to Mr. Justice Felix Frankfurter, who had been appointed to the United States Supreme Court in 1939 by President Franklin D. Roosevelt, after an outstanding career at the Harvard Law School. He died on February 22nd, 1965.

It would, however, give an incomplete picture of the contribution made to Anglo-American law by the leading Jewish jurists if I did not add as a supplement to this lecture a brief tribute which I paid in the Law Quarterly Review to F.F., as he was known to all his friends. It is too soon to attempt an appraisal of his contributions to the law, especially to the Constitutional Law of the United States, but I doubt whether any of the five men, whose lives are sketched in these pages, have played a greater or more permanent role in legal history than he has.

FIVE JEWISH LAWYERS
OF THE
COMMON LAW

THE JEWISH PEOPLE have always been known as The People Of The Law. The Old Testament is, as everyone knows, a repository of law, containing both legislative provisions and legal precedents. In his book on jurisprudence[1] Sir Frederick Pollock points out that Sir Edward Coke, the great Chief Justice, suggested in the preface to the Sixth Part of his Reports that Moses was the first law reporter: 'The reporting of particular cases or examples is the most perspicuous course of teaching, the right rule and reason of law: for so did Almighty God himself, when he delivered by Moses his judicial laws, exemplis docuit pro legibus, as it appeareth in Exodus, Leviticus, Numbers and Deuteronomy.'[2] Even more strictly legal is the Talmud, that vast storehouse of Jewish learning. Dr. David Daube of Cambridge University has shown in his recent studies how closely the work of the Talmudic scholars resembles that of the commentators on Roman Law.

It is not surprising therefore that the Jews have made important contributions to legal thought in most of the countries of the modern world. In evaluating this work

I

it must always be remembered that it has been done in little more than a century, because, even in so liberal a country as England, the Jews were excluded from the Bar and from the universities of Oxford and Cambridge until nearly the middle of the nineteenth century. In 1833 Sir Francis Henry Goldsmid was called to the Bar by Lincoln's Inn, but his call was by sufferance and not as of right.

In this lecture I have not time to speak of the contributions to legal learning which Jewish scholars have made in such countries as Germany[3] and Austria, France, and Italy, but every student of the law will be familiar with their work. They have been leaders especially in the fields of Roman law, legal philosophy, conflict of laws, and commercial law, and, strange to say, have been authorities also on canon law. Even if I were to limit myself to the common-law countries the field would be too wide to cover in a single lecture, for I should have to refer to the Dominions—to Australia and its great Chief Justice Isaacs, who also became Governor-General, and to New Zealand and its two Chief Justices Sir Arthur and Sir Michael Myers.

Tonight I shall speak of five men who, either in England or the United States, have played major roles in the history of the common law—they are Judah P. Benjamin, Sir George Jessel, Louis D. Brandeis, Rufus Isaacs, First Marquess of Reading, and Benjamin N. Cardozo. To this list it would have been natural for me to add the names of Arthur Cohen[4] Q.C., who was offered, when a Mem-

2

ber of Parliament, a High Court judgeship in 1881 by the Lord Chancellor, Lord Selborne, the offer being later withdrawn for political reasons as the Government did not wish to have a by-election, and of Irving Lehman,[5] Chief Judge of the New York Court of Appeals. But the career of Cohen was so predominantly forensic that it has tended to be forgotten, as the fame of a great advocate, like that of a great actor, is ephemeral in character, while Irving Lehman was my uncle, so that I should feel some diffidence in speaking about his work.

JUDAH PHILIP BENJAMIN[6]
1811—84

As I am speaking tonight of Anglo-American law, it is fitting that I should begin with a man whose strange and romantic career made him a leader both of the American and the English Bars, and Secretary of State of the Confederate States of America. If the American Civil War had turned out differently, as it easily might have done, the name of Judah P. Benjamin would have been one of the great ones of history: as it is, he is remembered to-day only by lawyers.

His father, Philip Benjamin, who was a native of the British island of Nevis in the West Indies, married Rebecca de Mendes in London about 1807. Shortly thereafter they set sail for the New World hoping to reach New Orleans, but it was learned that the Mississippi was blockaded by a British fleet, so their boat put into St. Croix, an island held by the British, although it was subsequently ceded to Denmark. Here Judah was born, a British subject, in 1811. Mrs. Benjamin had an uncle, Jacob Levy, who was a merchant at Wilmington, North Carolina, and as the prospects in the United States seemed brighter than in the Virgin Islands, the family left St. Croix in 1813. They eventually settled in Fayetteville, North Carolina, where Philip Benjamin continued his uniformly unsuccessful business career. His wife Rebecca was, however, 'resolved to hold her head high in spite of poverty' and she determined to send her son Judah to the Fayetteville Academy, which was one of the best schools in the South. Judah, under the guidance of his Scottish teacher, the Reverend Colin McIver, made such brilliant progress that in 1825, when only fourteen years old, he was sent to Yale University in New Haven, Connecticut, where many young Southerners completed their education in those days. Three years later he left without taking a degree owing to a 'violation of the laws of the college' as he put it in his letter of apology to President Day. More than thirty years later, in 1861, an Abolitionist journal charged that Benjamin had been forced to leave owing to dishonesty, but this accusation, which was not made until, owing to the secession of the Southern States, he could no longer defend himself, is in direct conflict with Benjamin's contemporary letter to the President in which he stated that his 'improper conduct' was not due to 'any premeditated disrespect' to any member of the Faculty. It would be odd indeed to speak of dishonesty as 'disrespect'.

In 1828, when he was only seventeen, Benjamin left North Carolina for New Orleans where he arrived with less than five dollars in his pocket. At that time there was a strikingly foreign air to this rapidly growing port, for a quarter of a century before it had belonged to the

French,[7] and the French influence remained an important one. To support himself, Judah took employment in a commercial house, the practical experience he then gained proving of the greatest value to him when, some years later, he became the leader of the commercial Bar. He was determined, however, to become a lawyer, and he succeeded in learning enough law in his spare time to make it possible for him to be admitted to the Bar in 1832, when he was only twenty-one. He must have been busy indeed at that time as he was also employed in giving English lessons to a young French girl, Natalie St. Martin, the daughter of an insurance company official who had fled from Santo Domingo during the slave insurrection. These lessons proved to be a disaster for Judah, because his pupil and he fell in love; they were married in 1833 when she was only sixteen. For ten years they lived an unhappy life together, but then she moved to Paris, where their daughter Ninette was born. They met only at intervals until they became reunited when Benjamin fled to Europe at the end of the Civil War. Perhaps part of his success in life may be ascribed to her extravagance because, although an indolent man by nature, he was driven to work hard to support his wife and daughter until almost the day of his death.

From the very beginning Benjamin's career as a lawyer was an outstanding success, for within three months of being admitted to the Bar he was arguing a case in the Louisiana Supreme Court. In 1834 he and Thomas Slidell, a friend from Yale, published a *Digest of the Reported De-*

cisions of the Superior Court of the Late Territory of Orleans and of the Supreme Court of Louisiana which immediately became a standard law book. The law of Louisiana was an odd amalgam of Roman, Spanish, French, and Anglo-American law, so that Benjamin had to acquire a wide knowledge of various legal systems which later proved invaluable to him when he wrote his classic work on the *Law of Sales*, and when he argued cases before the Judicial Committee of the Privy Council. Within ten years he had become the leading commercial lawyer in New Orleans. In 1842 he acquired a national reputation when he argued the cases which arose out of the mutiny of the slaves on the brig *Creole*.

In spite of his heavy law practice Benjamin decided in 1842 to go into politics, and after a brief campaign he was elected as a Whig to the Lower House of the State legislature. In 1844 he was one of the delegates to the Louisiana Constitutional Convention where he took particular interest in the founding of a State university. In 1852 he entered national politics when he was elected to the United States Senate. Before he could take his seat, in March 1853, President Fillmore nominated him as a Justice of the United States Supreme Court, the highest honour that had ever been received by a Jew, but he declined the offer as he preferred a more active political career.

Benjamin was not the first Jewish senator, as David Levy Yulee of Florida had been elected some years previously, but he was by far the most distinguished one who has ever sat in that body. As was inevitable, he was soon recognized to be one of the ablest members of the Senate, and by 1859 he was chairman of the Committee on Private Land Claims, and a member of the Judiciary Committee. Charles Sumner, the senator from Massachusetts who, as a strong Abolitionist, bitterly opposed all Southern senators, said that he considered him to be the most eloquent speaker in the Senate. At that time Senators were free to engage in private practice so that Benjamin was able to appear in a great number of cases before the United States Supreme Court, especially in those which involved questions of commercial and insurance law.

In 1861 Benjamin's career in the Senate came to an end. When Abraham Lincoln was elected President in November 1860, the Southern States made preparations to secede from the Union. On 31 December 1860 Benjamin delivered a speech in which he justified the doctrine of State rights, and urged that the parting between the Northern and the Southern States be in peace. On 4 February 1861, after Louisiana had seceded, he said farewell to the Senate in an oration which has been frequently quoted in the books. Sir George Cornewall Lewis, who was present, afterwards said: 'It is better than our Benjamin [Disraeli] could have done.'

As soon as the Southern Confederacy was founded, Benjamin, who was the outstanding Southern lawyer, was appointed Attorney-General by his friend President Jefferson Davis, who some years previously had been challenged to a duel by Benjamin when both were mem-

8

bers of the Senate. It is interesting to speculate that if Benjamin's advice had been taken by the Confederate cabinet before hostilities began, the South might have won the Civil War, because, as he foresaw that the coming conflict would be a long one, he urged the Government to ship 100,000 bales of cotton immediately to England, so as to buy arms and ammunition with the proceeds. It was the lack of arms which eventually was the main cause of the Southern defeat. His advice was, however, rejected, as his colleagues were convinced that the North would be beaten in a few months.

In September 1861 Benjamin was appointed Acting-Secretary of War and in November he received the full appointment. He held the office during six stormy months during which he reorganized the department, but some of the over-optimistic Confederate generals were opposed to his vigorous administration. The dissensions grew so bitter[8] that in March 1862 the President appointed Benjamin Secretary of State (Foreign Secretary), a post he held until the South finally collapsed. For the next three years he struggled desperately to obtain recognition for the Confederacy from Great Britain and France, and to get as much foreign aid as possible, but the European nations were cautious. In spite of the fact that Southern diplomacy was handicapped by the difficulty of communicating with its agents abroad, Benjamin was indefatigable in his negotiations, and at one moment when the Southern armies were in the ascendant, it seemed as if he might succeed. During the war years he was President

Davis's closest adviser, his cheerfulness and optimism tending to strengthen his gloomier and more temperamental leader. Many years later Davis described him as 'A master of law and the most accomplished statesman I have ever known', and, he added, 'My chief reliance among men'.[9]

On 2 April 1865, when the Southern cause was lost, President Davis, Benjamin, and some of the other members of the cabinet left Richmond, the Confederate capital, and a week later General Lee surrendered to Grant. It seemed probable that the leaders of the Confederacy would, if captured, be tried for treason and executed, so they decided to try to escape. Even now Benjamin remained as cheerful as ever; having decided that he would never be taken alive he ceased to worry about the future.[10] Travel on horseback proved too much, however, for one of his sedentary habits, so he and Davis agreed to part. Disguised as a Frenchman, he acquired a horse and waggon, crossed Georgia, and entered Florida where he hoped to find means of escaping by sea to the West Indies. He finally managed to hire a small fishing-boat which was stopped and searched by a Northern gunboat, Benjamin escaping capture by disguising himself as a cook. One of the searchers remarked that he had never before seen a Jewish cook on a boat, but nothing more was done about it. His dangers were not, however, ended, because the boat was nearly sunk in a storm before reaching the British Bimini Islands. He took a sloop from there but it foundered the next day, and he and three negroes had to escape in a skiff with a single oar. They were rescued by a British yacht, and later he reached Nassau. Then the boat on which he was sailing for England caught fire and only just succeeded in getting back to port. This was the end of his adventures because on 30 August 1865 he arrived in England, still buoyant and hopeful.

At fifty-four it is not easy for a man, who has just passed through four years of war, to begin a new career in a foreign country and under entirely strange conditions. For a moment Benjamin hesitated and thought of accepting a business post in Paris where his wife and daughter lived, but love of the law proved too strong and he became a student at Lincoln's Inn on 13 January 1866. Then the final blow fell as the little capital which he had in England was swept away when the banking firm of Overend, Gurney and Company failed. To keep himself going he became a leader writer for the *Daily Telegraph* at five pounds an article.

Benjamin became a pupil of Charles Pollock[11] who had a large mercantile practice. Although at first the Benchers of the Inn hesitated to grant him dispensation from the usual three years of studentship, they finally changed their minds,[12] and on 6 June 1866 he was called to the English Bar.

Benjamin joined the Northern Circuit, as Liverpool, through its cotton market, had close connexions with the South, but at first practice was slow in coming. His American accent and manners may have proved a hindrance, for he did not show the judges the deference which is customary in the English courts.[13] In 1867 his fees totalled only £493.12.6. In desperation Benjamin decided to become a legal author, and he spent all his spare time working on a law book. In August 1868 his *Treatise on the Law of Sale of Personal Property, with Reference to the American Decisions, to the French Code and Civil Law,* better known as *Benjamin on Sales,* was published; it was immediately recognized as the leading authority on the subject, and to this day it has maintained its reputation as a classic of English law. At that time there were few text-books that were more than annotated collections of cases, so that his emphasis on first principles and the clarity of his presentation were particularly striking. Moreover, his knowledge of foreign legal systems proved of special value in a branch of the law which is founded on the Law Merchant. From then on his career was meteoric. In 1870 he was made Queen's Counsel for the County Palatine of Lancaster,[14] but Lord Hatherley, then Lord Chancellor, refused his application in 1872 to become a full Queen's Counsel, apparently under the impression that such a step might antagonize public opinion in the United States. A few months later, however, his argument in the famous case of *Rankin* v. *Potter*[15] so impressed Lord Chancellor Hatherley that he gave him a patent of precedence. As these patents are almost unknown to-day it may be of interest to quote from Haydn's Book of Dignities:

From the time of George I, to the present day, the Crown has also on special occasions granted Patents of Precedence to eminent members of the bar, whether Sergeants, King's Counsel or ordinary Barristers, giving them certain rights of pre-audience over their fellows as fixed by their patents. Holders of Patents of Precedence have the same privileges as King's Counsel, but are able to hold briefs against the Crown, which a King's Counsel cannot do without a licence to plead.

Benjamin was never an outstanding 'jury' barrister, and, in spite of his quickness of mind, cross-examination did not come easily to him, so that with his increasing success he gave up his practice at *nisi prius*, appearing only in the House of Lords, the Privy Council, and the Court of Appeal. His great strength lay in constitutional, commercial, and maritime cases, and he became almost unrivalled in the Privy Council[16] where his knowledge of foreign legal systems proved to be of particular value. In 1877 he was counsel in thirty out of the sixty-five cases reported in the Appeal Cases for the House of Lords. It is interesting that his nearest rival that year was Arthur Cohen Q.C. In those days it was the custom to brief English barristers in Scottish appeal cases; Benjamin appeared in the majority of them, being helped by his knowledge of Roman law, which is the foundation of Scots law. Perhaps he may then have looked back with gratitude to the sound scholastic training he had received sixty years before from his first Scottish teacher.

The last dramatic incident in Benjamin's career occurred in 1881 in the House of Lords in *London and County Banking Co.* v. *Ratcliffe.*[17] In presenting the argument for the appellant, he stated a proposition of law with his usual confidence. One of the noble Lords—probably Lord Chancellor Selborne—remarked in a low voice 'Nonsense'. Benjamin stopped his argument, tied up his brief, bowed, and left the House.[18] The next day a conciliatory message was sent to him, and the incident was closed.

In the autumn of 1882 Benjamin, who had been injured in an accident, decided to retire from the Bar. Then came what *The Times* described as 'an event without parallel in the long history of the Bar', for on 30 June 1883 the Bench and Bar met in the Inner Temple Hall to give a dinner in his honour. In his speech the Lord Chancellor said that 'no man within my recollection has possessed greater learning or displayed greater shrewdness or ability, or greater zeal for the interests entrusted to him', and he spoke of his 'highest honour, united with the greatest kindness and generosity'. The Attorney-General, Sir Henry James, asked, 'Who is the man save this one of whom it can be said that he held conspicuous leadership at the Bar of two countries?' And he added, 'Rivalry with him seemed to create rather than disturb friendship.'[19]

When Judah P. Benjamin died in May 1884, *The Times* said in a leader:

His life was as various as an Eastern tale, and he carved out for himself by his own unaided exertions, not one but three several histories of great and well earned distinction. . . . No less inherited is that elastic resistance to evil fortune which preserved Mr. Benjamin's ancestors through a succession of exiles and plunderings, and reappeared in the Minister of the Confederate cause, together with the same refined apprehension of logical problems which informed the subtleties of the Talmud.

Benjamin was short, stout, and distinctly oriental in appearance. His most striking characteristics were his lively, amused eyes and his gentle silvery voice. He was not a great orator, but his mastery of general principles and his attractive lucidity often persuaded the Courts to accept his view of the law.[20] It has been said that he always had confidence in the assumption that it was the real business of the Judges to do what was fair and reasonable in the matter before them, and that he was disposed to assume that if prior decisions or technical rules stood in the way of this, then they must be modified or recast. He thus played an important part in helping to develop the English commercial law, and in preventing it from becoming rigid and stereotyped.

SIR GEORGE JESSEL[21]
1824—83

GEORGE JESSEL was born in London in 1824. Unlike the other four men whose careers I am sketching here, there is nothing striking about his life except its unbroken success. As his son Sir Charles Jessel has written: 'There was nothing romantic about my father's career to begin with. He had no struggle with poverty in early life. He lived in Savile Row and at a country house at Putney.' He was the youngest son of Zadok Jessel, a substantial merchant who also made a considerable fortune in the purchase of land. His education began at a school for Jewish boys conducted by Mr. Newmegen, who must have been a remarkable teacher, for many of his students made excellent records. At the age of sixteen Jessel matriculated at University College, University of London. In three years he took his B.A. degree with honours in mathematics, natural philosophy, vegetable physiology, and structural botany. The next year he took his M.A. degree, receiving a gold medal in mathematics and natural philosophy, and two years later he was elected to a Fellowship at University College. Jessel's scientific training proved of great value to him in his later life, and its influence may be seen in the clarity and simplicity of his judgements.

While still at the University, Jessel became a student at Lincoln's Inn, being called to the Bar in 1847. He read with Bellinger Brodie, the eminent conveyancer, and then became the pupil of E. J. Lloyd and of Sir Barnes Peacock; later he shared chambers in Stone Buildings with G. T. Jenkins. His success was immediate, for in his third year at the Bar he earned 795 guineas. Lord Bryce, in his sketch of Jessel, suggested that he got his start from Jewish solicitors, but Sir Charles Jessel wrote: 'No Jewish solicitor ever employed him till he had an extensive practice at the Bar, and in fact, in the early years of his professional career no Jewish solicitor could have kept a Chancery barrister even in wig powder.' After his initial success, Jessel's practice remained static for some years; he became so discouraged that he expressed the view that it would have been wiser for him to follow any other profession, but one day he was taken into Court and it then became clear that his strength lay in being an advocate rather than a conveyancer. He soon became the leading junior in the Rolls Court, and by the time he had reached the age of thirty-seven his practice was so large that he applied for silk. Lord Chancellor Westbury refused, however, to grant it to him, and it was not until 1865 that he became a Queen's Counsel and a Bencher of Lincoln's Inn.

In 1868 Jessel, who was a Liberal, was elected Member of Parliament for Dover. His style of oratory was too precise and dogmatic for him to become a popular speaker, but his speech on the Bankruptcy Bill so impressed Gladstone that in 1871 he offered him the post of Solicitor-General. In those days the Law Officers were free to engage in private practice, and during the two years in which he held office Jessel earned more than £29,000 per year. This did not prevent him from fulfilling his official duties most successfully: his advice, which was always clear and precise, was of particular help to the Cabinet which valued his definite answers to the questions submitted to him.[22] In 1873 Lord Romilly, the Master of the Rolls in whose Court Jessel had established complete ascendancy, retired, and Jessel, after some delay, was appointed to succeed him. He then began a judicial career which has been equalled by few men.

At that time the Master of the Rolls, who was third in the judicial hierarchy after the Lord Chancellor and the Lord Chief Justice, was an *ex officio* member of the Court of Appeal, but his chief function was to sit as a Judge of first instance in the Rolls Court. It was here that Jessel made his greatest contribution to English law, because during the eight years in which he sat in that Court, he was given an opportunity of dealing with almost every phase of equity. When he died *The Times* said: 'Probably no tribunal of first instance ever gave greater satisfaction than the Rolls Court during the eight years which he presided over it. Arguments were short. Appeals were rare, for his decisions were unerring as they were expedicious.' The rapidity with which he worked enabled him to deliver an astonishing number of judgements. In the library of Lincoln's Inn there is an unpublished manuscript, *Index to the Decisions, Dicta, Judgements and Observations of Sir George Jessel, Master of the Rolls, 1873–1883*, by Henry Rae-Arnot, LL.D. Under the letter A there are references to 126 cases which were reported either in one of the various law reports or which were mentioned in the newspapers, so that some idea can be gathered of the total number of judgements he must have delivered. If the *Index* were published it would fill more than 500 pages. The speed with which he did his work may be ascribed to his clarity of mind, which enabled him to strike immediately at the heart of any problem, and to his self-confidence which kept him from hesitating when once he had made up his mind. His characteristic saying, 'I may be wrong, and sometimes am, but I never have any doubts'[23] is illustrated by the number of his judgements which begin with such phrases as 'To my mind the matter is very plain and clear', or 'I have no hesitation in making a precedent'. As a Judge of first instance Jessel never once reserved judgement, not even in the famous *Epping Forest Case* (*Commissioners of Sewers* v. *Glasse*).[24] In that case, which occupied twenty-three days in Court, more than 100 witnesses were called, statutes extending back to the time of King John were cited, and documents were piled on documents: nevertheless Jessel delivered his sixteen-page oral judgement immediately on the conclusion of counsel's arguments. No better illustration of his method can be cited than this case, for it shows with what skill he was able to analyse the complicated facts, and how clearly,

in short staccato sentences, he was able to state his conclusions.

Perhaps the chief—perhaps the only criticism—that
was advanced against Jessel as a Judge was that he was so
quick in seizing the point of a case that he did not give
counsel sufficient time in which to develop their arguments. This habit once gave rise to a famous scene which
Atlay has described in his sketch of Lord Chancellor Herschell in his *Lives of the Victorian Chancellors*:[25] 'When he
[Herschell] was at the Bar, Sir George Jessel once at-
tempted to cut him short in an argument. Herschell, who
was not a man to be set down, retorted on the Master of
the Rolls, that, important as it was that people should
get justice, it was even more important that they should
be made to feel and see that they were getting it.' It is interesting to note that Farrer Herschell was a Jew by race;
his father Haim Herschell, who had been born in Prussian
Poland, changed his Jewish faith and took the Christian
name of Ridley when he emigrated to England. Here he
took a leading part in founding the British Society for the
Propagation of the Gospel among the Jews, and later
married a Miss Mowbray. Their son Farrer was educated
at University College, London University, a generation
after Jessel, and he then became a student at Lincoln's
Inn. In 1872 Herschell was made a Queen's Counsel a
month after Judah Benjamin had received his Patent of
Precedence, so that they ranked next each other. In 1874
Herschell, a Liberal, was elected a Member of Parliament
and in 1880 he was appointed Solicitor-General. When

Jessel died in 1883 Herschell declined the offer of the Mastership of the Rolls, but in 1886 he accepted the Lord Chancellorship. He remained Chancellor for only six months as Gladstone's ministry soon fell, but he held office again from 1892 to 1895. He died on a mission in Washington in 1899. It is interesting that Benjamin, Jessel, and Herschell were all Benchers of Lincoln's Inn at the same time, but there does not seem to have been any particular friendship between them.

In 1881 Jessel ceased to be a Judge of first instance and thereafter sat only in the Court of Appeal. The story, as told by his son, is an interesting footnote to English legal history.

It was entirely owing to my father's position that the Master of the Rolls became a permanent Judge of the Court of Appeal. In 1881 Lord Justice James died, and there was no one of sufficient weight in the Court of Appeal to hear appeals from a man like Sir George Jessel. It was therefore much to his regret that it became necessary to pass a special Act of Parliament by which the Master of the Rolls ceased to be a judge of first instance, and though he had up to that date been *ex officio* a member of the Court of Appeal, he now became permanently a judge in that Court.

Unfortunately Jessel only served as President of the Court of Appeal for two years, as he died on 23 March 1883, discharging his duties with his usual thoroughness to the very end. In a leader the next day, *The Times* said that, 'he was one of the greatest English Judges, possessed of a very genius for the work of the Bench', and it pointed out that 'it was his unique distinction that he was one of the most erudite of case lawyers and also the most courageous of Judges in handling authorities. . . . Unlike the ordinary authority-monger, he was the master, not the slave of precedents.'

Jessel's fame is secure as one of the great creative Judges of English legal history. He consciously modified the law when he felt that the old rules were no longer in accord with modern conditions, and his example encouraged other Judges to get rid of dead timber. The raciness of his style added great strength to his judgements, for it gave them a sense of reality which a more ponderous and learned judgement sometimes lacks. Such phrases as 'counsel searching for authority for lack of argument', 'a man is allowed by law to be a fool if he likes', and 'vultures feeding upon expiring copyrights' are found again and again in his pages. Jessel once said, half in jest, that he considered Lord Hardwicke the greatest of equity Judges, Lord Cairns second, and himself third. He excluded Lord Eldon, whom he called 'the dubitative Chancellor' from the list because he could never make up his mind. That Jessel was right in ranking himself as one of the great equity Judges cannot be open to doubt: the only question is whether he was not the greatest of them all.

It may be of interest to note that Jessel was the first Jew who, as Solicitor-General, took a share in the executive government of his country, the first Jew sworn as a regular member of the Privy Council, and the first Jew who took a seat on the Judicial Bench.

Apart from his strictly judicial work, Jessel had many other interests. As a member of the committee empowered to make rules for the Supreme Court under the Judicature Acts he played a leading part in making the new system work. He was *ex officio* one of the commissioners of patents under the Patent Law Amendment Act 1852, and from 1873 to 1883 he was, in fact, the working head of the Patent Office. Here his early scientific training proved of particular value. Jessel was one of the few Judges who have ever been Fellows of the Royal Society. Perhaps his greatest interest was in education, and especially in the University of London. As Vice-Chancellor from 1881 until his death he took an active part in its management, introducing some useful reforms.

Jessel had dark hair, grey eyes, a straight nose, and a somewhat large mouth. He was physically indolent, but in argument his face 'became wonderfully animated'. His bust has been placed in the lobby of the Royal Courts of Justice as a memorial to one of England's greatest Judges.

LOUIS D. BRANDEIS
1856–1941[26]

T HE PARENTS of Louis Brandeis left Czechoslovakia, which was then part of Austria, in 1849 as they were Liberals and dreaded the reaction which would follow the revolution of 1848. When they reached America they travelled west, first to Madison, Indiana, and then, after two years, to Louisville, Kentucky. It was there that the youngest of their four children—Louis Dembitz Brandeis—was born 13 November 1856. As his father had become a prosperous grain merchant, Louis was given every educational advantage, and in his sixteenth year he was awarded a gold medal 'for pre-eminence in all his studies' by the Public Schools in Louisville. In 1872 the family went to Europe for a visit, but they/ remained there for three years, during part of which Louis attended the Annen-Realschule in Dresden. Perhaps it was here that he acquired that thoroughness and care for detail which characterized his work throughout his life. In 1875, when the Brandeis family returned to America, Louis entered the Harvard Law School where the famous 'case system' of teaching law had recently been established. The 'intellectual self-reliance and spirit of in-

24

vestigation' which this inductive method engendered appealed to the young law student who made a scholastic record which has remained unequalled to the present day. One of his friends wrote: 'The professors listen to his opinion with the greatest deference, and it is generally correct'—a comment which was as much a tribute to the professors as it was to the brilliant but uncomfortable young law student.[27] At that time Brandeis kept a notebook in which he quoted from Emerson: 'A foolish consistency is the hobgoblin of little minds', and from Lowell: 'The foolish and the dead alone never change their opinion.' In his later life it was the capacity to accept new ideas which distinguished Brandeis from his more conservative fellow lawyers. On the other hand his intensely realistic nature made him describe Plato's Republic as 'the most theoretically nonsensical plan that human ingenuity ever invented'.

On graduation Brandeis moved to St. Louis, and in November 1878 he was admitted to the Missouri Bar. Two years later he returned to Boston to become a partner of his Harvard classmate Samuel D. Warren Jr. It was then that he first met Oliver Wendell Holmes Jr. who was later to become the famous Justice of the United States Supreme Court. The young firm prospered, but Brandeis was not too busy to give a course in Evidence at the Harvard Law School in 1883. His father wrote to him that this was 'the greatest honor that can be given to a young man of your age', and he added, 'I simply cannot help being aware that the profession of an academic teacher and possibly a writer is the most satisfying and desirable, and it may have been imprudent on my part to have expressed my opinion so unreservedly'.[28] The next year Brandeis was offered a professorship, but, after some hesitation, he refused it as he preferred the active life of the Bar.[29] Again his father wrote to him: 'Perhaps I could be called a coward for taking so little pleasure in a struggle, and I probably should congratulate myself that my sons are made out of better metal. I think that I have tried all my life to do my duty, and this sense of duty my sons have inherited from me.' It was this sense of duty which later impelled his son to follow a course which was unpopular with his friends and which estranged him from many of his legal colleagues. His father added: 'Fortunately the love of a struggle and a little ambition is given to them as their maternal inheritance, and therefore they are so truly every inch men—may God help them.'[30]

The last quarter of the nineteenth century was a period of remarkable expansion in American industrial life during which the great mergers and trusts were founded. It was also a time of industrial unrest, which culminated in the terrible steel strike at Homestead, Pennsylvania, in 1890, when the strikers and the hired strike-breakers engaged in a pitched battle. Later Brandeis wrote: 'I think it was the affair at Homestead which first set me to thinking seriously about the labor problem. It took the shock of that battle, where organized capital hired a private army to shoot at organized labor for resisting an arbitrary cut in wages, to turn my mind definitely toward a searching study of the relations of labor to industry.'

Public sentiment against this industrial anarchy began to develop at that time, with the result that in 1887 Congress passed the Inter-State Commerce Act which was followed in 1890 by the Sherman Anti-Trust Act. Legislation proved, however, to be in large part an ineffective weapon because the courts held that a number of statutes enacted by Congress and by the State legislatures were unconstitutional, and others were construed in a narrow spirit. The large corporations employed the ablest lawyers to block most of the attempts to control their activities, it being then that the term 'corporation lawyer' was coined. Brandeis described the situation in these words: 'The leaders of the Bar, without any preconceived intent on their part, and rather as an incident to their professional standing, have, with rare exceptions, been ranged on the side of the corporations, and the people have been represented, in the main, by men of very meagre legal ability. If these problems (regulations of trusts, fixing of railway rates, the relations of capital and labor, etc.) are to be settled right, this condition cannot continue.' Brandeis, who did not underrate his own ability, determined to become 'the people's lawyer', and to fight case after case without reward. This did not prevent him, however, from carrying on a large and lucrative private practice. He planned every minute of his time, because he felt that time was the one thing which must never be wasted.[31]

It would be wearisome to describe the cases in which Brandeis was engaged for they have long since been dead and buried, but two are of special importance. From 1906 to 1914 he fought the New York, New Haven, and Hartford Railway, which was attempting to establish complete control over all traffic in the New England States, until finally in 1914 the company capitulated. The other case was *Muller* v. *Oregon*, decided by the Supreme Court in 1910.[32] A law enacted by the State of Oregon limiting the working time of women to ten hours a day was attacked as being unconstitutional as an unreasonable interference with the workers' right to freedom of contract. Brandeis, who appeared in defence of the law, submitted a written brief (as the printed submissions are called in the United States) in which he devoted only two pages to the legal argument but more than a hundred pages to a masterly statement of the evidence showing the evil consequences of overwork on women. The Supreme Court, which had struck down much social legislation, in this case upheld the law.

The importance of Brandeis's work cannot be judged, however, merely by the cases he won. Of greater importance was his influence on the general thought of his time and on the young men who became his disciples. Outside the courts he fought his crusade in lectures, articles, and books, his most famous book, published in 1914, being entitled *Other People's Money and How the Bankers Use It*. In it he attacked 'the control which a few financiers exercise over the capital of America', and he argued that 'the fetters which bind the people are forged from the people's own gold'. It was words such as these which played a large part in bringing about the democratic revolution in thought which, after the reaction of the Coolidge–Hoover generation, proved to be the intellectual foundation of the New Deal. Some critics accused Brandeis of unduly seeking publicity, but this is an unfair judgement because he felt that law was not something to be confined to the court-room, and that it was the duty of the lawyers to instruct and to lead public opinion. 'All law', he wrote, 'is a dead letter without public opinion behind it, but law and public opinion interact and they are both capable of being made. Most of the world is in more or less a hypnotic state, and it is comparatively easy to make people believe anything, particularly the right.'

In 1912 when Woodrow Wilson was elected President, it was thought probable that he would appoint Brandeis his attorney-general, but at the last moment, in the interest of party harmony, he chose James C. McReynolds, who later, as Mr. Justice McReynolds, became the symbol of reaction and bigotry. Brandeis, who never wore gloves when he fought his battles, had made many enemies,[33] and they now felt that he had been safely eliminated from public life. But on 28 January 1916 the sudden blow fell: President Wilson nominated Louis D. Brandeis to be an Associate Justice of the United States Supreme Court.

Under the Constitution of the United States the President nominates a Justice of the Supreme Court, but the

consent of the Senate is required before the nomination
can become effective. Occasionally this consent has been
refused, and in the case of Brandeis it seemed particularly doubtful whether he would receive the necessary
confirmation. For five months the Judiciary Committee
of the Senate held hearings, at which various lawyers with
whom he had clashed gave evidence against him, but
finally it reported in his favour. On 1 June 1916 his
nomination was confirmed by the Senate by forty-seven
votes to twenty-two, and the first Jew took his seat on
the Supreme Court.

When Brandeis became a Justice, the great majority
of the nine Justices were conservative in outlook. The
most important function of the Supreme Court is to de-
clare whether statutes enacted by the Federal legislature
(Congress) or by the legislatures of the forty-eight States
are constitutional. In many instances this is in essence a
political rather than a legal question, especially where
the XIVth Amendment is concerned because this pro-
vides that no State shall 'deprive any person of life,
liberty or property without due process of law'. As the
Supreme Court has held that any statute which is unreasonable or unfair constitutes such a deprivation and is
therefore unconstitutional, it has enabled the Judges to
hold that legislation of which they disapprove is invalid.
This they have done in the best of faith because it is
natural for a man to believe that any law with which he
disagrees must be contrary to reason. Mr. Justice Holmes,
who had been appointed to the Supreme Court in 1902,

was the first to attack this attitude of mind: in his famous dissents he argued that all life was built on experiment and that the legislatures should not be prevented from experimenting unless it was certain that no reasonable person could have reached the same conclusion. When Brandeis became a member of the Court he joined Holmes in his dissents, but instead of appealing to the liberal scepticism which was the basis of Holmes's philosophy, he founded his judgements on the positive ground that the political and economic views of the majority of the Judges were out of date.[34] He felt that because the law had got out of touch with contemporary facts it no longer commanded the confidence of the people: 'to secure respect for law, we must make the law respectable.' He concluded that 'a lawyer who has not studied economics and sociology is very apt to become a public enemy', and so he filled his judgements with statistics and with references to non-legal sources. It is probably true that no other man has so influenced the teaching of law at the universities as has Brandeis, for the legal curriculum which used to be limited to the study of cases has been widened to include a study of the facts of economic life, and the social philosophy on which the cases are based. It is therefore Brandeis's method, rather than the particular views which he expressed, which is important, for it is doubtful whether his conception of society, with his emphasis on the individual, is in accord with the trend of present-day thought. With some truth Brandeis has been described as the last of the nineteenth-century

Liberals. He disliked the 'bigness' of contemporary life which, he believed, was crushing the individuality of the ordinary man.[35]

It is not possible to analyse here in any detail the more than 600 judgements which Brandeis delivered during the twenty-three years in which he served on the Bench. For most of those years he was in the minority, but it must be remembered that in the United States the Supreme Court is not absolutely bound by its own previous decisions so that the views of the Court may gradually be altered. That has happened since Holmes and Brandeis raised the standard of liberalism, for it is true to say that to-day their ideas have triumphed. Two of his dissents may be cited here because they illustrate both his social philosophy and his judicial method.

In *Hitchman Coal & Coke Company* v. *Mitchell* (1917)[36] the plaintiff company in West Virginia operated its 'non-union' mine under an agreement with its employees that they would not join the United Mine Workers of America, and that, if they did, their employment should cease. The U.M.W., which was strong in the adjoining States, sent representatives who sought to persuade the plaintiff's employees to agree to join the Union. This did not involve any incitement to break existing contracts as the employment was 'at will'. On these facts the majority of the Supreme Court upheld the decree of the District Court under which the officers of the Union were enjoined, *inter alia*, from 'knowingly and wilfully enticing plaintiff's employees, present or future, to leave plaintiff's service on the ground that the plaintiff does not recognize the United Mine Workers of America or runs a non-union mine, etc.'. Mr. Justice Pitney, who delivered the opinion of the court, said:[37] 'In short, plaintiff was and is entitled to the good will of its employees, precisely as a merchant is entitled to the good will of his customers although they are under no obligation to continue to deal with him', and that the conduct of the defendants 'exceeds the bounds of fair play'. In support of this conclusion he cited, with considerable courage, a dictum from Bowen L.J.'s judgement in the *Mogul Steamship Case*,[38] although that case would seem to be authority for exactly the opposite conclusion.

Brandeis J. dissented, Holmes J. and Clarke J. concurring in this dissent. Without any attempt at literary ornamentation he answered in brief paragraphs each point made in the majority opinion. On the main issue he said:[39]

The purpose of interfering was confessedly in order to strengthen the union, in the belief that thereby the condition of workmen engaged in mining would be improved; the bargaining power of the individual workingman was to be strengthened by collective bargaining; and collective bargaining was to be ensured by obtaining the union agreement. It should not, at this day, be doubted that to induce workingmen to leave or not to enter an employment in order to advance such a purpose is justifiable when the workmen are not bound by contract to remain in such employment.

It seems surprising that this conclusion should ever have been doubted.

An even more interesting case is *New State Ice Co.* v. *Liebmann* (1931).[40] An Oklahoma statute declared that the manufacture, sale, and distribution of ice was a public business, and forbade anyone to engage in it without first having procured a licence from a State commission. The majority of the Supreme Court held that the statute was unconstitutional as it was repugnant to the due process clause of the XIVth Amendment in[41] 'unreasonably curtailing the common right to engage in a lawful private business'. The Court reached the conclusion that:[42] 'We are not able to see anything peculiar in the business here in question which distinguishes it from ordinary manufacture and production.'

Brandeis's dissent, in which Stone J. (later Chief Justice) concurred, occupied more than thirty pages with elaborate footnotes. He held that the conception of a public utility was not static, and that the question whether the local conditions were such as to justify converting a private business into a public one was a matter primarily for the determination of the State legislature. He then proceeded to analyse in detail the conditions in Oklahoma, including the climate, the number of household refrigerators, and the distribution of ice plants. Although Brandeis disliked monopolies, he held that in certain circumstances it might be desirable for the State to curtail competition, especially if there was a danger that the whole industry would suffer by a wasteful duplication of plants. He said:[43]

The people of the United States are now [1931] confronted

with an emergency more serious than war. Misery is wide-spread, in a time not of scarcity, but of over-abundance. . . . Some people believe that the existing conditions threaten even the stability of the capitalistic system. . . . (M)any persons think that one of the major contributing causes has been unbridled competition. . . . The discoveries in physical science, the triumphs in invention, attest the value of the process of trial and error. In large measure, these advances have been due to experimentation. . . . There must be power in the States and the Nation to remold, through experimentation, our economic practices and institutions to meet changing social and economic needs. . . . It is one of the happy incidents of the federal system that a single courageous State may, if its citizens choose, serve as a laboratory; and try novel and economic experiments without risk to the rest of the country. . . . If we would guide by the light of reason, we must let our minds be bold.

A year later Franklin D. Roosevelt was elected President of the United States, and the greatest experiment in social and economic history—the New Deal—was introduced by minds that were bold and not afraid of fear. For the next four years the Conservative majority of the Court struck down much of this New Deal legislation while Brandeis continued to dissent, but suddenly the picture changed and he found that the ideas, which had been regarded as dangerous and revolutionary when Holmes and he had first advocated them, were now recognized as reasonable and necessary. The old Judge saw that his prophecies had become acceptable in his own country.

On 13 February 1939, in his eighty-third year, Brandeis felt that his work was completed so he sent his resignation to his friend President Roosevelt whose ideas of government, especially in regard to the control of capital and of investments, had in many ways been developed under the influence of the liberal Justice. Perhaps the tribute which pleased him most was the letter of farewell which he received from his fellow Justices: 'Your long practical experience and intimate knowledge of affairs, the wide range of your researches and your grasp of the most difficult problems, together with your power of analysis and your thoroughness in exposition, have made your judicial career one of extraordinary distinction and far-reaching influence.' Less than two years after his resignation, on 6 October 1941, Mr. Justice Brandeis died.

No sketch of Brandeis would be complete without a reference to Zionism, because, next to the law, this was the major concern of the later years of his life. Until he was more than fifty he had shown little interest in Jewish affairs and none at all in the Jewish religion. Then in 1912 after he met Jacob De Haas, who had been associated with Theodor Herzl in London, he became converted to the Zionist cause. In 1914 he became chairman of the Provisional Executive Committee for General Zionist Affairs which was established in New York. During the war he kept in close touch with Dr. Weizmann in England, and he welcomed the Balfour Declaration. After the war a difference concerning policy separated Weizmann and Brandeis, with the result that in 1921 the latter resigned as an active leader of the movement; he remained, however, an enthusiastic Zionist to the day of his death.

As this paper is concerned with Anglo-American law it may be of interest to note Brandeis's enthusiasm for English Judges and for English political and legal institutions. It was to Sir George Jessel that he turned for his model Judge when he wrote:[44] 'Knowledge of decisions and powers of logic are mere handmaidens—they are servants, not masters. The controlling force is the deep knowledge of human necessities. It was this which made Jessel the great lawyer and the greater judge.' To the English political system he paid this tribute in 1920:[45]

England is nearer civilization than any other country. That it is nearer democracy seems clear. As I watch events from day to day I am ever more impressed with the existence of a potent public opinion—expressing itself manfully and with much immediate effect. Our own machinery—referendum, initiative, primary elections, and elective officials galore—is a miserable substitute for the alert, intelligent watchfulness which is reflected generally in the press and which finds, in the interrogations in the House of Commons and in letters to *The Times*, the means of uncovering wrong action before it has become irremediable or has ceased to be of moment.[46]

It was often said that Brandeis resembled Abraham Lincoln, and the Justice, who had a considerable element of vanity in his character, took a secret pride in the comparison, but, judging from the photographs of Lincoln, the resemblance did not go very deep. Both were tall, both were angular, both had deeply lined faces, and both had sensitive mobile mouths, but it was in their eyes that they differed, for Lincoln's were filled with sorrow and compassion, while Brandeis's grey-blue eyes, especially at moments of excitement, were bright with restless curiosity. It would be wrong to picture him as a great prophet or a great leader or as a great scholar, for he was none of these: he will be remembered rather as a man who refused to be bound by the traditional prejudices of the past, and who believed with all his heart that intelligence and a clear understanding of facts were essential if we were to build a better world for the future. He was a courageous man, and he therefore advocated courageous action. He had little sympathy with those who were afraid to make experiments or to change the traditional ways of life. For him the United States represented 'the great experiment', and he taught that true Americanism was based on a belief in the principles of freedom and equality which had guided the forefathers of the nation.

RUFUS ISAACS, FIRST MARQUESS
OF READING
1860—1934[47]

At the end of the seventeenth century Michael Isaacs settled in Essex, but at the beginning of the nineteenth century his descendants decided to move to Aldgate in London where they founded the firm of M. Isaacs & Sons, fruit merchants. It was then that another Michael Isaacs married Sarah Mendoza, one of whose ancestors was an official of the famous Spanish and Portuguese synagogue in Bevis Marks whose history is connected with that of Disraeli and of Judah P. Benjamin. (It may be noted that the famous prize-fighter Daniel Mendoza (1765–1836) was one of Sarah's relations.) They had a number of children, including Henry Isaacs, who became Lord Mayor of London in 1889, and Joseph Michael (born 1832) who married Sarah Davis in 1855.

In 1860 Joseph and Sarah's second son was born at 3 Bury Street, St. Mary Axe, and was named Rufus Daniel after his maternal uncle. Rufus's school career seems to have been as varied as it was turbulent. 'He was the terror of his schoolmasters, the scandal of the neighbourhood and the despair of his father.' At the age of four he and his older brother Harry were sent to a school at Gravesend and then were taken to Brussels where Rufus's wonderful memory first impressed his teachers.[48] In other ways he was a less satisfactory pupil, and to the relief of his Belgian headmaster he was brought back to Mr. Mendes's school in London when he was eight. At the age of thirteen he went to University College School where the headmaster predicted that Rufus would have a distinguished career if he went to the Bar. His scholastic interests were, however, so limited that the next year he was removed from school and was set to work in the family business. He was too restless to settle down there, so in 1876 his father took him to Cardiff to sign on as ship's boy on the *Blair Athole*, which was about to sail for South America and India. The popular story that he ran away from home is unfortunately a myth. In 1877 the ship's boy had his first glimpse of India as the ship entered the Hooghly: forty-four years later he took the Royal salute in those waters as Viceroy of India.

When the *Blair Athole* returned to England in 1877, Rufus left the sea for ever, and entered the family business for a brief period, but three years later, in 1880, he became a member of the Stock Exchange. His inexperience and over-optimism caused him to be hammered in 1884, so that at the age of twenty-four he was a ruined man saddled with debts. He decided to leave England and go to South America, but then came the strangest incident in his strange career. He had said good-bye to his family and was at the station waiting to take the train to Liverpool, when his brother arrived breathlessly to tell him that his mother was ill and that he must return home. Sarah Isaacs was a remarkable woman: she fostered the theory that she was delicate, and she managed to have hysterics whenever it became necessary to get her way. To avoid trouble, her husband, who was of a cheerful nature, instructed his children that 'if your mother says it is so, it is so, even if it isn't so'. Now, at the crucial moment, Mrs. Isaacs remembered the prophetic words of the headmaster of University College School, so she determined that her son should go to the Bar instead of seeking his fortune abroad. And to the Bar he went, being admitted a student by the Middle Temple in 1885. At last Rufus had found the profession for which he was destined, and during the next three years he set himself to the study of law. He became the pupil of Sir Henry Poland, who had a large and varied common law practice, and of Lawson Walton, who was destined to lead him in the famous case of *Allen* v. *Flood*[49] in 1895. Having been called to the Bar in December, 1877, he immediately received a brief in *Young* v. *Isaacs*, a case in which his father's firm were the defendants. It is interesting that the young junior appearing for the plaintiff in that case was J. A. Hamilton, later the great Lord Sumner. Isaacs's career began auspiciously, for in his second year he earned £750, but then it hung fire for a short period during which he gained experience in the County Courts and the City of London Court. The pause was only a brief one as it soon became recognized that he was one of the ablest juniors at the Bar. Although he appeared in many of the most famous cases of the period—and in the years before 1914 the newspapers were filled with the reports of libel and divorce cases which the public read with avid interest—it was especially in commercial litigation that he made his reputation. It was in them that his ability to analyse the most involved situations and to deal with complicated figures proved of particular value. He was never a dramatic or 'showy' advocate—his strength lay in the patient and inexorable marshalling of facts.

In 1898 at the age of thirty-seven Isaacs took silk, and soon established himself as the outstanding leader in the Commercial Court which had been instituted in 1895 with Mr. Justice Mathew as the presiding Judge. The efficiency and lack of technicalities in that court well suited Isaacs's informal style of advocacy. After less than five years as a King's Counsel he was earning more than £14,000 a year. His strong constitution enabled him to do with only five hours' sleep: it was his practice to rise between four and five in the morning to read his briefs and prepare his arguments. He once said: 'The Bar is never a bed of roses. It is either all bed and no roses, or all roses and no bed.'

In 1904 Isaacs led for the prosecution in his most famous case and the one which finally established his reputation—the prosecution of Whitaker Wright, the financier. W.W., as he was popularly known, had gone to the United States when twenty-one, and in ten years he had made £200,000 in his deals in mining shares. He returned to London in 1889 where he founded the London and Globe Finance Corporation and various other companies which had boards composed of distinguished and noble directors who were completely dominated by him. For a time everything seemed to prosper, but in 1901 the whole financial structure collapsed. The disappointed shareholders demanded a prosecution, but the Attorney-General, Sir Robert Finlay, refused to authorize one as he felt that it had no reasonable prospect of success. After a long delay a private prosecution was undertaken in 1903, Wright being indicted on twenty-six counts. He then made the fatal error of fleeing to the United States, but he was recognized there and brought back to England after lengthy extradition proceedings. The trial began on 11 January 1904 and lasted for twelve days. It was at first believed that no jury would be able to follow the complicated figures that were involved in the various balance sheets, but gradually Isaacs established his case. The highlight of the trial came during the three days of Wright's cross-examination which, built up step by step, finally broke his self-assured defence. He was found guilty and sentenced to penal servitude for seven years, but before he could be taken to prison he swallowed a tablet of cyanide of potassium which he had concealed in his mouth during the final day of the trial, and fell dead in an ante-room of the court.

A few months after the Wright trial, Isaacs was elected as a Liberal Member of Parliament for Reading at a by-election. At first he played only a minor role in the House, but after the General Election in 1906, when the Liberals swept the country, he took a leading part in the debate on the Trades Disputes Bill as he had an intimate knowledge of trade union law. The purpose of the Bill was to reverse the law as it had been established by the House of Lords in the *Taff Vale*[50] case, which the trade unionists felt was a threat to their existence.

In March 1910 the Solicitor-General, Sir Samuel Evans, resigned, and Isaacs was appointed to the office which Sir George Jessel had filled thirty-nine years before. Seven months later the Attorney-General, Sir William Robson, resigned on being appointed a Lord of Appeal, and Rufus Isaacs became Attorney-General and head of the English Bar.

As Attorney-General, Isaacs represented the Crown in a number of important cases, but the one which will be longest remembered was the trial of the Seddons for the murder of Miss Barrow, who lived with them, by poisoning. Anyone wishing to study his style of advocacy ought to read the record of that trial, because his cross-examination of Seddon is a masterpiece of clarity and tact. Never once did he attempt to bully the witness or to take an unfair advantage of him, but gradually he made it clear that Seddon was the cold and greedy type of man who would be prepared to commit murder for a few hundred pounds.[51]

In 1913 the Attorney-General was himself on the defensive, because it was then that the so-called Marconi 'scandal' threatened him with political and professional ruin. It has often been said that lawyers make the worst witnesses and to this rule Rufus Isaacs was no exception, because a little more candour at the beginning of the proceedings would have dispelled much of the suspicion which later became attached to the simple facts of that case. In 1910, Godfrey Isaacs, Rufus's younger brother, who was managing director of the English Marconi's Wireless Telegraph Co. Ltd., began negotiations with the Government to erect eighteen wireless stations throughout the Empire. The whole matter was referred to the Imperial Wireless Committee which reported in favour of the Marconi Co. as against the Paulsen system. On 13 February 1912 the Marconi Company sent in a tender which was accepted by the Government on 7 March.

At this time there was in the United States the separate American Marconi Company, just as there were four other separate Marconi Companies in other foreign countries. The American company had not been a success, so early in 1912 steps to reorganize it were taken, including the issue of 1,400,000 new 5-dollar shares. As the English company had a large interest in the American company (although the American had none in the English company), Godfrey Isaacs agreed to be responsible for placing 500,000 shares. He had 100,000 shares left when on 9 April 1912 he suggested to his brothers Rufus and Harry to take some of the American shares. Rufus refused, but his brother Harry took 50,000. A week later

Rufus unfortunately changed his mind, and bought 10,000 shares from Harry at the market price. On the same day Rufus Isaacs sold 1,000 shares each to Mr. Lloyd George, the Chancellor of the Exchequer, and to the Master of Elibank, the Liberal Chief Whip. The shares rose in value for a time, but eventually, when they were all sold, the net result was a loss of £1,300 on the transaction. In accordance with his invariable practice the whole of these transactions were carried out in Rufus's own name.

In July 1912 a formal contract between the English Company and the British Government was concluded, but when the contract came before the House of Commons for ratification on 7 August, it was attacked as being too favourable to the English Marconi Company, and the matter was adjourned until the autumn. In October the Government moved for the appointment of a Select Committee of Inquiry; in the course of the debate both Lloyd George and Rufus Isaacs denied that they had any interest, direct or indirect, in the English company, but they made no reference to the shares which they had purchased in the American company. From the strictly legal standpoint their failure to refer to the American company was justified, as the American company had no interest in the English company and could in no way benefit from the contract, but from the wider standpoint it nearly proved fatal because when the facts were stated by Rufus Isaacs in a libel action against a French newspaper six months later, the greatest suspicion was aroused. Isaacs and Lloyd George then gave evidence before the Select Committee which issued majority and minority reports on 13 June. Both reports were in agreement that the Ministers had not been guilty of corruption, but while the majority report contained no criticism of their actions, the minority report said that in the circumstances the purchase of the American shares had been improper and that the Ministers had been 'wanting in frankness and respect for the House of Commons' in the October debate. Thereupon an official motion of censure upon the Ministers concerned was moved on behalf of the Opposition, but it was defeated by a majority after both the Ministers had spoken. No one studying the facts to-day, now that all party passions have disappeared, can have any doubt concerning the honesty and good faith of the Ministers because, to put the argument on the lowest ground, it is inconceivable that a man who was earning £30,000 a year would have openly entered on a corrupt transaction which at best would have yielded him a profit less than he could have earned in a single week at the Bar, and which, if discovered, would mean complete ruin; on the other hand it was unfortunate that the facts were not disclosed at the earliest opportunity. It is difficult to believe that if Isaacs had been advising any one else he would not have told him that that was not only the right, but also the wisest, thing to do.

In October 1913 Lord Alverstone resigned as Lord Chief Justice, and Rufus Isaacs was appointed to succeed him. It has been suggested that in view of the criticisms to which the Marconi case had given rise he ought not to have accepted the appointment, but a refusal on his part would have been to some degree an acknowledgement that the charges that had been brought against him were justified. It is fortunate that he decided as he did, because otherwise the country would have been deprived of the great services which he rendered during the years to come.

Lord Reading, as Rufus Isaacs had then become, had only a brief and interrupted judicial career, for when war came in 1914, although he continued to hold his judicial office, he was increasingly called on to serve in other fields. In 1915 he was sent to the United States as head of an Anglo-French mission to raise a loan of £100,000,000. He proved to be so popular that when in 1917 it became necessary to send a new British ambassador to Washington he went there as Special Envoy and High Commissioner. On his return to England in 1919 he resumed his judicial office, but he served for less than two years. In January 1921 he accepted the responsible and difficult post of Viceroy of India. Thus, after thirty-seven years, his legal career came to an end.

Lord Reading's term as Viceroy ended in 1926, and on his return to England he was made a Marquess, the highest rank of nobility ever attained by a Jew. In 1931 he was appointed Foreign Secretary in the so-called National Government, but he relinquished the post after the General Election at the end of that year. Three years later in 1934 he died in London.

It is as an advocate, and not as a Judge, that Lord Reading will always be remembered by lawyers. He lived in an age of giants—Carson, Simon, and F. E. Smith—and I remember the heated arguments we used to have when I was a young law student in 1913 as to which one of the four was the greatest. It was generally agreed that in cases which required the clear analysis of difficult financial and commercial problems Rufus Isaacs had no equal. He was hardly given an opportunity to prove his qualities as a Judge, but it is doubtful whether he would ever have become a great one for he did not have the philosophic and scholarly type of mind which is an essential basis for the highest judicial work. He was at his best as a Judge of first instance, because he was able to make clear to the jury the questions they had to answer. His most famous case was the trial at Bar of Sir Roger Casement for high treason.[52] The Lord Chief Justice's charge to the jury has been described as a model of fairness. There are not many of his reported judgements, but they show that he placed the primary emphasis on common sense rather than on technical rules of law.

No sketch of Rufus Isaacs would be adequate without a reference to his extraordinary good looks. He has been described as 'a dark Apollo'. As a boy he had been a powerful athlete, his skill as a boxer serving him well when he was sailing on the *Blair Athole*; in later life his strong constitution enabled him to do work which would have exhausted an ordinary man. A sense of humour is not an essential part of the successful barrister's equipment, but Rufus Isaacs's quiet but caustic wit helped to illuminate some of his most striking cross-examinations. He used words like a rapier, and it is perhaps as a great legal fencer—cool, graceful, strong, and accurate—that he can best be pictured.

BENJAMIN NATHAN CARDOZO
1871—1938[53]

Benjamin Cardozo's life began in the shadow of a tragedy and ended with such honour and distinction as few men have ever attained. The Cardozo family, as the name shows, originally came from Portugal, but after the expulsion of the Jews they went to Holland, and from there they later moved to England. About 1752 Aaron Nunez Cardozo came to the Colonies where he married a daughter of Moses Seixas, founder of the Bank of Rhode Island, and a soldier in the Revolution. Their son Michael was nominated for Justice of the Supreme Court of New York State, but he died before the election took place. His son was Albert Cardozo, who, as a very young man, showed brilliant promise. At that time in the middle of the century New York politics were controlled by Tammany Hall, which was under the rule of the notorious Boss Tweed. In 1862 he offered a judgeship to Albert who had not the strength of character to refuse it although he must have known that it meant subservience to the political machine. It is unlikely that he ever accepted a bribe, but there can be no question that he granted favours to the Tammany boss. His appointment of a receiver for the Erie Railroad was such an open scandal that an investigation was thereupon begun by the Judiciary Committee of the State Assembly. Albert Cardozo resigned in 1874 before the investigation was concluded, an act which was construed as an acknowledgement of guilt. He returned to practise at the Bar, but he never recovered from the disgrace which clung to his name. He died, a broken man, in 1885.

His second son, Benjamin, born on 24 May 1870 in New York City, was brought up in the shadow which had fallen on the family, and there can be no doubt that it was the ambition of his life to wipe out his father's shame. Only once or twice did he refer to it when speaking to his most intimate friends, but his feelings on the subject were so well known that no one ever referred to his father or to the Tweed ring in his presence. When he was only nine his mother, whom he adored, died, and his older sister Nell took charge of her brothers and sisters. The devotion between the brother and the sister continued unbroken until the day of her death.

As a child Benjamin was taught by a tutor, Horatio Alger, who later became famous as the author of the most popular boys' books of the period, in all of which the hero triumphed over poverty and adversity by courage and hard work. It is highly probable that his tutor's heroes played a part in moulding Benjamin's character. It was also Alger who helped to develop in him his love for English literature, which later found expression in his judgements and in his legal essays.

At the end of his fifteenth year Cardozo became the youngest student at Columbia University. The shy, reserved little boy soon showed that he was a brilliant scholar, but the modesty, which distinguished him all his life, made him popular with his fellow students. When he graduated with the highest honours at the age of nineteen he was elected Vice-President for life by the men of his class (in the United States 'years' are known as 'classes'), and was chosen to be the class orator at the Commencement exercises.[54] In his address, which was entitled *The Altruist in Politics*, he attacked the unrealistic altruists who were advocating an absolute community and equality of wealth. In the concluding paragraph he said:

In almost every phase of life, this doctrine of the political altruists is equally impracticable and pernicious. In its social results it involves the substitution of the community in the family's present position. In its political aspect it involves the absolute dominion of the State over the actions and the property of its subjects. Thus, though claiming to be an exaltation of the so-called natural rights of liberty and equality, it is in reality their emphatic debasement. It teaches that thoughtless docility is a recompence for stunted enterprise. It magnifies material good at the cost of every rational endowment.

In this essay he referred to Matthew Arnold's doctrine which stressed the value of individual energy and which emphasized 'the instinct of expansion as a factor in human progress'. Arnold, who to-day is hardly read, was one of the chief formative influences in the development of Cardozo's philosophy of life.

After graduation Cardozo spent two years at the Columbia University Law School, and was then admitted to the New York Bar. He became a partner of his older brother Albert Cardozo, Jr., who died in 1909; before his death they had joined the firm of Simpson and Werner, which had thereupon been re-named Simpson, Werner and Cardozo. In his practice Cardozo became more and more what is known in the United States as a lawyers' lawyer because whenever a particularly difficult question of law arose other lawyers tended to call him into consultation. He spent his spare time in writing his first book, *The Jurisdiction of the Court of Appeals of the State of New York*, published in 1904, which remains the authoritative work on the subject.

In 1913 a wave of long-needed reform struck New York City, and, as a result, various groups formed the Fusion party to oppose the Tammany candidates.[55] In New York State the Supreme Court Judges, who are Judges of first instance, are elected by popular vote, so a strong committee under the chairmanship of Charles C. Burlingham, one of the most distinguished lawyers in the history of the New York Bar, asked Cardozo to let them put forward his name. He did so with some reluctance, and with some surprise he found himself elected. He had barely commenced his judicial duties when, a month later, Governor Glynn designated him to serve on the Court of Appeals, the highest Court in the State. For eighteen years he was a member of that Court, and during the last five of them he was the Chief Judge.[56] It is generally recognized that during those years the New York Court of Appeals was the strongest Court in the United States, and that its judgements have had an important influence on the development of the common law throughout the nation. It must be remembered that the United States Supreme Court is primarily concerned with the constitutionality of statutes and with the interpretation of Federal Acts, the decision of common law cases being for the most part in the hands of the State Courts.

In the past fifty years there have been two American Judges who have been recognized as being pre-eminent: Mr. Justice Holmes and Chief Judge Cardozo. Holmes, who first made his reputation as a great legal scholar with the publication of his classic book, *The Common Law*, will always be remembered for his judgements in cases concerned with Constitutional law, while Cardozo will be regarded as the great interpreter of the common law. It is not by chance that Holmes is always compared with Chief Justice Marshall, the most famous of all Constitutional lawyers, while Cardozo is bracketed with Joseph Story. Cardozo had all the qualities which are the mark of a great common law Judge: the sense of history which enables the Judge to understand the reasons which gave birth to the rule and the various influences which have affected its development, the sense of philosophy which enables him to see the particular rule, not as a separate and individual provision, but as part of a more general legal principle, and the sense of reality which will encourage him so to adapt the experience of the past that it may best serve the needs of the present. It would require a volume to show how completely Cardozo's judgements meet these tests, but I can only refer to two of his judgements which have had a direct influence on English as well as on American law.

In *MacPherson* v. *Buick Motor Co.* (1916)[57] Cardozo delivered an opinion which has probably had more influence on the development of the law of torts than any other judgement since *Rylands* v. *Fletcher*.[58] The defendant, a manufacturer of motor-cars, sold a car to a retail dealer who resold it to the plaintiff. While the plaintiff was driving in the car one of the wheels, made of defective wood, collapsed, and he was injured. The defendant argued that, although it owed a duty of care to the dealer, it owed none to the plaintiff. This argument was dismissed by Cardozo in the following words:

> The dealer was indeed the one person of whom it might be said with some approach to certainty that by him the car would not be used. Yet the defendant would have us say that he was the one person whom it was under a legal duty to protect. The law does not lead us to so inconsequent a conclusion. Precedents drawn from the days of travel by stage coach do not fit the conditions of travel today. The principle that the danger must be imminent does not change, but the things subject to the principle do change. They are whatever the needs of life in a developing civilization require them to be.

Sixteen years later, in *Donoghue* v. *Stevenson*,[59] the House of Lords held by a majority of three to two that a manufacturer of ginger-beer, who had sold a bottle with a dead snail in it to a retailer, was liable for this negligence to a third person who had consumed the ginger-beer. The majority judgements cited Cardozo's judgement in the *MacPherson* case with approval, and in distinguishing previous English decisions they adopted the arguments he had used. These two cases are of major importance, not only because of the particular point at issue, but especially because they showed that the law was capable of growth, and need not be limited by precedents first established in the stage-coach days.

Second only in importance to the *MacPherson* case was his judgement in *Wagner* v. *International Railway Co.* (1922).[60] Owing to the negligence of the Railway Company the plaintiff's cousin had fallen from the platform of a train when it was crossing a trestle bridge. The plaintiff, in an attempt to rescue his cousin, walked back along the bridge in the dark, slipped, and was badly injured. The defendant argued that it owed no duty of care to the plaintiff as he was a volunteer when seeking to rescue his cousin. Judge Cardozo said:

> Danger invites rescue. The cry of distress is the summons to relief. The law does not ignore these reactions of the mind in tracing conduct to its consequences. It recognizes them as normal. It places their effects within the range of the natural and the probable. The wrong that imperils life is a wrong to the imperilled victim; it is a wrong also to his rescuer.

Thirteen years later, in *Haynes* v. *Harwood* [1935],[61] the English Court of Appeal had to determine whether a police constable who, to save a woman and some children, had stopped the defendant's horses which had run away owing to the driver's negligence, was entitled to recover damages for the serious injuries he had suffered. The Court of Appeal, reversing the trial judgement, held that the plaintiff was entitled to do so, and in reaching this conclusion it cited the *Wagner* case. Here again a narrow interpretation of the law was displaced by a more liberal doctrine which brought the law into consonance with the principles of humanity.[62]

In 1920 Cardozo was invited to deliver the Storrs lectures at Yale University, later published under the title of *The Nature of the Judicial Process*. The extraordinary success of this slight volume was due in part to the charm of the author's style, and in part to the fact that in it, for the first time, a great Judge gave a careful analysis of the various considerations, both conscious and unconscious, which influence a Judge in reaching his conclusions. It has been said that genius consists in the ability to make clear the obvious which has never been understood before, and in this sense Cardozo's lectures are a work of genius. They contain no strikingly new ideas when taken separately, but as an analysis of the judicial process as a whole they give us a picture which is unequalled in legal literature. The case method of teaching law had fostered the idea that this process consisted solely in logical deductions from established premisses, but Cardozo showed how inadequate this interpretation was, and by doing so he helped to give a new orientation to legal scholarship both in America and in England. His words gave encouragement to those who thought of the common law not as a static collection of rules inherited from the past, but as a living body of principles capable of growth and change.

As the years have gone by [he wrote] and as I have reflected more and more upon the nature of the judicial process, I have become reconciled to the uncertainty, because I have grown to see it as inevitable. I have grown to see that the process in its highest reaches is not discovery, but creation; and that the doubts and misgivings, the hopes and fears, are part of the travail of mind, the pangs of death and the pangs of birth, in which principles that have served their day expire, and new principles are born.[63]

Three years later Cardozo gave a second series of lectures entitled *The Growth of the Law*, which he described as a supplement to his first book. In them he again emphasized that no single approach would give us the correct answer to our legal problems: 'We are not to bow down before our metaphysical conception or our historic datum, and shut our eyes to living needs, and yet we are not to find a living need in every gust of fancy that would blow to earth the patterns of history and reason.'[64]

In 1928 Cardozo published *The Paradoxes of Legal Science*, in which he discussed the relation between justice and law. Again he emphasized that the legal process must be one of compromise and concordance. He concluded that: 'The reconciliation of the irreconcilable, the merger of antitheses, the synthesis of opposites, these are the great problems of the law.'[65] His many references in these lectures to Greek philosophy show how great a part his early classical training played in the formation of his ideas; in relating his general principles to the concrete cases which, in his words, he used as a kind of legal litmus paper, he was a true Aristotelian.

His last book, *Law and Literature*, published in 1930, was a collection of various essays and addresses. In the title essay he described, in a passage which has frequently been quoted, the various types of judgements:

As I search the archives of my memory, I seem to discern six types or methods which divide themselves from one another with measurable distinctness. There is the type magisterial or imperative; the type laconic or sententious; the type conversational or homely; the type refined or artificial, smelling of the lamp, verging at times upon preciosity or euphuism; the type demonstrative or persuasive; and finally the type tonsorial or agglutinative, so called from the shears and the pastepot which are its implements and emblem.

In this essay the majority of his quotations are taken from English judgements ranging over many centuries, and of them he says: 'For quotable good things, for pregnant aphorisms, for touchstones of ready application, the opinions of the English judges are a mine of instruction and a treasury of joy.'

In 1932 Mr. Justice Holmes, who had reached the age of ninety, resigned from the United States Supreme Court, and it therefore fell to President Hoover, a conservative Republican, to appoint his successor. There were already two Judges (Chief Justice Hughes and Mr. Justice Stone) from New York on that Court, and it rarely happens that two Judges from one State are appointed. Moreover, Mr. Justice Brandeis was a member of the Court, and there were some bigots who were bitterly opposed to the elevation of a second Jew. But the lawyers throughout the United States were in agreement that Cardozo was the fittest man to succeed 'the great Dissenter',[66] and, what was even more striking, this demand was echoed by the ordinary man in the street. It is not often that a Judge, especially a Judge who is essentially a scholar, captures the imagination of the people, but Cardozo had become for them the symbol of justice—of justice based on law but which refused to be bound by the fetters of the past. On 15 February 1932 the President sent Cardozo's nomination to the Senate and in less than a month it was confirmed unanimously.

Cardozo served on the Supreme Court for six years. They were the most controversial six years in the history of the Court because, during the first period, the majority of the Justices held that a large part of the New Deal legislation was unconstitutional, while, in the second, a new and more liberal constitutional doctrine was followed. Even though his own views finally prevailed, the controversy on the Court saddened Cardozo, who had felt far happier when, as Chief Judge of the New York Court of Appeals, he had helped to create a spirit of unity in his Court which has rarely been equalled. Powerful and convincing as his Supreme Court opinions were, they seemed to lack some of the fire and genius which make his common law judgements such an outstanding contribution to the history of the law. It is as a common lawyer, in the great tradition, that he will always be remembered.

In May 1938, at the end of the Court year, Cardozo left

Washington, and came, a dying man, to the home of Judge Lehman at Port Chester. It was fitting that he should spend the last two months of his life with his closest friend, with whom he had worked side by side for many years. He died on 9 July 1938.

When the Inner Temple library was destroyed in a 1940 air raid Judge Cardozo's executors presented his library to the Inn as a memorial to a man who had made so great a contribution to the common law and who had often expressed so sincere an affection and admiration for this country. His portrait has been placed on the bookplate, but it can give only an inadequate idea of his beautiful sensitive face. Although there was not a trace of weakness about him, he had an almost feminine charm. He gave one, in an indefinable way, a feeling that here was a man who, without losing his humanity and sympathy, represented in his life the highest ideals that a man can hold. It is necessary to say this because otherwise it is not possible to understand all that he meant to the people of his country. Cardozo was a great lawyer, but he was an even greater man.

At the exercises held in his memory in the Supreme Court, Chief Justice Hughes said:

His gentleness and self-restraint, his ineffable charm, combined with his alertness and mental strength, made him a unique personality. With us who had the privilege of daily association there will ever abide the precious memory not only of the work of a great jurist but of companionship with a beautiful spirit, an extraordinary combination of grace and power.[67]

CONCLUSION

In summing up the characteristics of the five men whose lives have been briefly sketched here, I think that we can properly emphasize the following qualities they had in common.

The first point to notice is the fundamental liberalism of the five men. No one of them was a revolutionary in the sense that he wished to destroy or even to alter in any radical degree the great system of law which he was helping to administer, but, on the other hand, no one of them was prepared to accept the established rules merely because they had been long established. They felt that they could best serve the law by criticizing those parts of it which were no longer consonant with the needs of contemporary society. I have always felt that the Jews, belonging as they do to a minority group, can best fulfil the function of the constructive critic: they are less conditioned, to use a psychological phrase, than other men to accept things as they are. This is one reason why they suffer from a lack of popularity; because the critic, although playing an essential role in any country which is not to succumb to gradual atrophy, is always regarded with suspicion and sometimes with dislike.

The second quality which we find is clarity of thought. Jessel's judgements are an outstanding illustration of this, for there is not a single vague or woolly sentence to be found in any of them. To paraphrase his own words, they may very occasionally be wrong but they are never uncertain. The same is true of Brandeis, and to only a lesser degree of Cardozo because once or twice his sense of literature—we can call it his sense of poetry—led him to use phrases which are so gracefully fashioned that their meaning, when carefully analysed, is not immediately clear. You may have noticed how insistent all the five men were on the need for establishing the facts in every case: this is a truism which every lawyer is taught but which many forget. This emphasis on facts is seen, perhaps, most strikingly in Lord Reading's career at the Bar. He did not rely on eloquence or on an appeal to the emotions: thus it was his relentless analysis of the details of the balance sheets which finally convicted Whitaker Wright.[68] It is worth noting that none of the five showed the least tendency towards histrionic exaggeration which is sometimes—I believe mistakenly—said to be a Jewish characteristic.

The third quality is the interest in scholarship which they showed throughout their lives. With the exception of Lord Reading—and he frequently expressed regret at the opportunities which he had failed to take—each of them was a scholar of the first rank. At school and at the university they showed the qualities which were later to make them the intellectual leaders of their generation.

This belief in, and devotion to, scholarship has been re-cognized as a Jewish attribute so that it is not surprising to find that it contributed so much to the lives of these Jewish lawyers.

In one of his essays Sir Frederick Pollock lauded what he described as 'judicial valour'. I think that it is true to say that each of these men had that intellectual courage without which no great work can be accomplished. Per-haps we can see that best illustrated in the varied life of Judah Benjamin for he was always ready to face every new problem cheerfully and with confidence in his own strength. It takes moral courage to begin a new career at the age of fifty-four.

May I make one final point? It is a striking thing that the mother played a dominant role in the life of four of the five men who are described here. Benjamin's father, who failed in everything he tried, left it to his wife to hold the family together. Brandeis's father was a charming and a high-principled man, but he was essentially a dreamer: it was to his mother that Brandeis always turned for ad-vice, and it was from her that he inherited his ambition and his driving force. It was Lord Reading's mother who, at the very last moment, kept her son from emigrating, and who insisted on his taking up a legal career. It was Cardozo's mother who instilled in her son that devotion to the finer things in life which may be said to have marked his every act. I have in my rooms at Oxford the books which she gave him when he was a little boy—the books which taught him that love of English literature which later moulded the style of his judgements. Those books he kept until he died. It is more than a coincidence that in each of these four instances the mother should have so greatly influenced her son—it is an illustration of the part which women play in Jewish family life.

I hope that in this paper I have not been unduly chauvinistic, but at a time in the world's history when the Jews have been criticized and attacked in many countries, I do not think it is improper to point out how great a contribution they have made to one of the major forces of civilization—the English Common Law. In an address to the New York County Lawyers Chief Judge Cardozo said: [69]

The tradition, the ennobling tradition, though it be myth as well as verity, that surrounds as with an aura the profession of the law, is the bond between its members and one of the great concerns of man, the cause of justice upon earth. Like the old charter extorted by the barons, the body of our law when we read it line upon line may smack of mere antiquities, the customs of a vanished past. The myth, however, is still there, the myth of a great bible, the myth of mighty tablets hewn and hammered out by successive generations of advocates and judges under the imperious drive of a passion to shape the forms of justice.

This passion to shape the forms of justice has been one of the dominant forces in the life of the Jewish people from the time of the mighty tablets to the days in which we now live, and it is therefore not surprising to find that the five Jewish lawyers I have here described have played their part in 'the ennobling tradition of the law'.

NOTES

1. *A First Book of Jurisprudence*, 5th ed., p. 291.

2. In his report of *Ratcliffe Ca.*, 3 Rep. 40 a, b, Coke refers to the case of the daughters of Zelophehad, narrated at the beginning of the twenty-seventh chapter of the Book of Numbers. He adds that 'this case seemed of great difficulty to Moses, and therefore, for the deciding of that question, Moses consulted with God'.

3. Seven names which every legal scholar will recognize are Friedrich Julius Stahl, Heinrich Dernburg, Otto Lenel, Paul Laband, Georg Jellinek, Eugen Ehrlich, and Hermann Kantorowicz.

4. Arthur Cohen, nephew of Sir Moses Montefiore, was born in 1829. As a child he showed marked mathematical ability. Owing to his religion it was difficult for him to enter Cambridge University, but the Prince Consort, who was then the Chancellor of the University, secured his admission to Magdalene as a Fellow Commoner in 1849. He qualified for a degree, being placed as fifth wrangler, but he was not able to take it until 1858 owing to the Test Acts. While at Cambridge he was President of the Union Society in 1853. He was called to the Bar in 1857, where he rapidly acquired a large practice, chiefly in commercial and international law. In 1872 he was junior counsel to the Attorney-General, Sir Roundell Palmer (afterwards the Earl of Selborne, L.C.) in the *Alabama* arbitration. In 1874 he became a Queen's Counsel, and in 1880 he entered Parliament, defeating Sir Edward Clarke. His nephew, Lord Justice Cohen, in his Presidential Address in 1947 to the Jewish Historical Society of England, said concerning the offer of a judgeship: 'In February 1881, the expected offer came from the Lord Chancellor, Lord Selborne, but it was withdrawn as the Liberal Party feared an election in the borough owing to its instability in party politics. Sir William Harcourt, whom he had consulted as to whether he should accept, had told him that if he should decide to refuse the judgeship in order to devote himself for the time being to politics, he could always be certain of another at a later date. That he ought to receive a renewal of the offer was certainly the view o f his colleagues at the Bar and of Judges on the Bench, but

the assurance was not realized and the omission led to the witticism of Mathew, L.J., who said—"'What can Cohen expect of Herschell except a Passover ?".' In 1905 Cohen was appointed a Privy Councillor. He died in 1914. In a tribute to him in the *Law Quarterly Review* (January 1915) his friend Professor Dicey said: 'One must go back for a parallel to names almost prehistoric to our younger lawyers. Cohen was the peer of Sergeant Maynard and Plowden, or, in a branch of the law remote from his own, the great conveyancers of the early nineteenth century.'

5. Irving Lehman was born in New York City in 1876. He studied at Columbia University, receiving his B.A. in 1896 and his LL.B. in 1898. He practised law from 1898 to 1908 when he was elected a Justice of the Supreme Court of the State of New York. In 1923 he was elected an Associate Judge of the Court of Appeals. He was elected Chief Judge in 1939, holding office until his death in 1945. For a number of years while he was Chief Judge his brother Herbert was Governor of the State. In an appreciation of his work in the 1947 *Menorah Journal* Mr. Justice Shientag wrote: 'He possessed the qualities of a great judge; intellectual and moral integrity, wisdom, discipline, courage, imagination and a passion for truth. Devotion to duty and a deep sense of responsibility were the hallmarks of his character.'

6. The most recent book on Benjamin is *Judah P. Benjamin: Confederate Statesman*, by Robert D. Meade. Copyright 1943, by Oxford University Press, Inc., New York. I am indebted to it for many of my quotations. There are numerous references to him in Jefferson Davis's *Rise and Fall of the Confederate Government*. There are brief biographies in the *Dictionary of National Biography*, and in the *Encyclopaedia Britannica*, and articles in *The Times* and in various magazines.

7. New Orleans was purchased from Napoleon in 1803 as part of the famous Louisiana Purchase. In 1830 it had a population of nearly 50,000; by 1840 it exceeded 100,000.

8. In February 1862 the Federal forces under General Burnside captured Roanoke Island off North Carolina. General Wise, who was in command of the Confederate troops on the Island, blamed the Secretary of War for not sending him sufficient reinforcements. Professor Meade has written a valuable analysis of this dispute, pp. 219–30.

9. Meade, p. 3.

10. Meade quotes (p. 316) the following passage from Burton Harrison's 'The Capture of Jefferson Davis' in *Century*, 1883: 'While his companions were perfectly silent, Benjamin's silvery voice was presently heard as he rhythmically intoned for their comfort verse after verse of Tennyson's *Ode on the Death of the Duke of Wellington*. As long as Benjamin remained with them his cheerfulness and

NOTES

adaptability to emergencies made him a most agreeable comrade.' Benjamin's·
choice of enlivening poetry emphasizes the originality of his character.

11. Charles Edward Pollock (1823–97) was the fourth son of Sir Jonathan
Frederick Pollock, Lord Chief Baron of the Exchequer for nearly a quarter of
a century. He was made a Baron of the Exchequer in 1873. In 1876 he tried the
case of *Regina* v. *Keyn* (13 Cox Crim. Cases 403) in which the master of the *Fran-
conia* was charged with manslaughter. This was one of the few criminal cases in
which Benjamin appeared as counsel.

12. Lord Cairns was particularly influential in this matter.

13. Sir Henry James, who always befriended Benjamin, advised him early in
his career that he must not suggest to the Judges that their knowledge of the
law was inferior to his own.

14. 'Palatine Silks' no longer exist. Concerning their history Sir Malcolm
Macnaghten has written (1949, 65 *Law Quarterly Review* 91): 'Before the pass-
ing of the Judicature Acts, 1873, the Duchy of Lancaster used to appoint two
members of the Outer Bar to be "Palatine Silks", and in addition to the two
appointed by the Duchy the senior judge of assize on the Northern Circuit used
to appoint Palatine Silks. Section 73 of the Judicature Act, 1873, expressly
preserved the precedence of those who were "Palatine Silks" when the Act
was passed. The archives of the Duchy contain one at least of the Letters Patent
sealed by the Duchy creating a "Palatine Silk" before ever Benjamin came to
England.'

15. (1873) VI Eng. & Irish App. Cas. 83. In this case Benjamin led Arthur
Cohen. It concerned loss of freight occasioned by perils of the sea, and notice
of abandonment.

16. He described the Privy Council as 'the court above all others in Christen-
dom in which one can practice law like a gentleman'. (Meade, p. 372.)

17. (1880–1) 6 App. Cas. 722.

18. Davey, Q.C., who was with Benjamin for the appellant, was allowed to
make the reply the next day.

19. In his amusing *Bench and Bar* (3rd ed. 1891), Serjeant Robinson wrote
(p. 163): 'A cynic might suggest that the Bar, at least, were glad to commem-
morate the departure of so formidable a competitor from amongst them; but no
one who knew the sentiments entertained by the profession towards Benjamin
would think so.'

20. Professor Meade (p. 372) quotes from the memoirs of Gustavus Wald,
a distinguished Cincinnati lawyer, who heard Benjamin present an argument in
the Privy Council: 'English lawyers are much less emphatic and vehement in
argument before a court than are American lawyers. But no lawyer whom I

heard in England was so absolutely impersonal as Benjamin. On both occasions that I heard him he seemed not to represent his client, but abstract justice, the law. . . . As he spoke all uncertainty seemed to vanish; there appeared to be but one view which could in reason be accepted, and that view was presented so simply and clearly that it seemed that any boy of ten could not fail to grasp it.' Benjamin's arguments were unusually brief and compressed. It has been suggested that this was due to his experience in the American courts where the time allotted to counsel is strictly limited.

21. No full-length biography of Jessel has been published. There are notices of him in the *Dictionary of National Biography* and in the *Encyclopaedia Britannica*. Lord Bryce referred to him in his *Studies in Contemporary Biography* (1903). His son Sir Charles Jessel published an article entitled 'An Eminent Victorian Lawyer' in *Blackwood's Magazine* (1926).

22. He took a leading part in the preparation of the famous Geneva arbitration between Great Britain and the United States concerning the arming of the Confederate raider *Alabama*.

23. Sir Charles Jessel wrote: 'The Attorney-General while Sir George Jessel was Solicitor-General was Sir John Duke Coleridge, afterwards Lord Coleridge. It is to this period that the "never doubt" story belongs. Lord James of Hereford told me that Coleridge had told him that when he was Attorney-General and my father Solicitor-General they were both called into consultation by the Cabinet with reference to the *Alabama* claims. Before they went in Coleridge asked my father for his opinion on some point, an opinion which my father had no hesitation in giving, whereupon Coleridge said to him, "Have you any doubts about it, Jessel ?". "My dear Coleridge", replied my father, according to Coleridge's version to Lord James, "I may be wrong, and often am, but I never doubt." Lord James afterwards met my father and asked him if the story were true, upon which my father answered, "Very likely, but Coleridge, with his constitutional inaccuracy, has told it wrong. I can never have said "OFTEN WRONG".'

24. (1874–5) 19 Eq. 134.

25. Vol. ii, p. 460.

26. The primary authority on Brandeis is the 700-page volume *Brandeis, A Free Man's Life* by Alpheus Thomas Mason (1946). The Viking Press: New York.

27. Two of the professors were Bradley and Ames. Of them Brandeis wrote: 'Whatever is "against conscience" is to him [Bradley] the subject of abhorrence. He desires that there should be no distinction between what is "legally right" and what is "morally right". Ames is like the inflexible professor of the deductive method, who being timidly informed that his principles, if carried out, would split the world to pieces, answered carelessly: "Let it split; there are enough more planets" ' (Mason, p. 37).

28. Ibid., p. 66.

29. He continued, however, to show a keen interest in academic law. In 1887 he helped in the foundation of the *Harvard Law Review*, becoming one of the trustees and its first treasurer. In 1890 Brandeis and Warren published in the Review an article entitled 'The Right to Privacy'. Dean Roscoe Pound has said that this article did 'nothing less than add a chapter to our law'. The right to privacy is not recognized by the English law, but some cases come perilously near to doing so.

30. One cannot help feeling that Brandeis's father had a more lovable, and perhaps a finer, character than did his son. When he first came to the United States he wrote: 'I already love our new country so much that I rejoice when I can sing its praises. . . . I have gotten hold of a book which contains the messages of all the Presidents. This week I have been reading of the progress made in Washington's day, and I felt as proud and happy about it as though it had all been my own doing. . . . Afterwards I laughed at myself, but there is something in it. It is the triumph of man which emerges, and in which we rejoice. I feel my patriotism growing every day, because every day I learn to know the splendid institutions of this country better' (Mason, p. 16).

31. When Brandeis died in 1941 he left an estate of over $3,000,000. This was due in part to the frugal manner of his life, for he lived an almost Spartan existence.

32. 1910, 208 U.S. 412.

33. Professor Mason has said (op. cit., p. 3): 'In working up his cases, whether private or public, he seized every opportunity to probe more deeply than the immediate litigation seemed to require. Often that was how he won his cases—by putting the human before the legal element. Thus he often roused personal enmity and baffled both friend and foe. His opponents started by hating his tactics and ended by hating the man himself.'

34. Judge Cardozo contrasted their points of view in these words: 'Brandeis has thought out a pattern for the whole universe, and he has a niche into which every fact fits. . . . Holmes didn't see any pattern to the universe' (George S. Hellman, *Benjamin N. Cardozo*, p. 274).

35. Mason, p. 354: 'Anything big, simply because it was big, seemed to be good and great. We are now coming to see that big things may be very bad and mean. . . . When you increase your business to a very great extent, and the multitude of problems increase with its growth, you will find, in the first place, that the man at the head has a diminishing knowledge of the facts, and, in the second place, a diminishing opportunity of exercising a careful judgment upon them. Furthermore—and this is one of the most important grounds of the in-

efficiency of large institutions—there develops a centrifugal force greater than the centripetal force. Demoralization sets in; a condition of lessened efficiency presents itself. . . . These are disadvantages that attend bigness.'

36. (1917) 245 U.S. 229.

37. At p. 252.

38. *Mogul Steamship Co.* v. *McGregor, Gow & Co.* (1889) 23 Q.B.D. 598.

39. At p. 273.

40. (1931) 285 U.S. 262.

41. At p. 278.

42. At p. 279.

43. Pp. 306–11.

44. Mason, p. 80.

45. Ibid., p. 529.

46. In 1940 he told the British ambassador in Washington that Great Britain must remain the mandatory for Palestine, 'because of the character of her people, the experience of her government, and the possession by the English of the knowledge essential to a practical undertaking; because of her record in respect to Jews; and the absence there of anti-semitism as contrasted with France as exhibited in the Dreyfus incident' (ibid., p. 595).

47. A complete biography entitled *Rufus Isaacs, First Marquess of Reading*, written by his son the present Lord Reading, has been published in two volumes, 1942 and 1945 (Hutchinson).

48. It is my belief that modern educationalists underrate the importance of a good memory. In such a subject as law it may prove invaluable. It enabled Rufus Isaacs to conduct long and intricate cross-examinations without consulting any notes.

49. This was one of the famous conspiracy cases relating to trade unions. It was heard in the House of Lords in 1897, reported in [1898] A.C. 1. In this case Cohen Q.C. led for the appellant.

50. In *Taff Vale Ry.* v. *Amalgamated Society of Railway Servants* [1901] A.C. 426 the House of Lords held that an action in tort could be brought against a trade union in its registered name.

51. Seddon's cross-examination began as follows:
Attorney-General: 'Miss Barrow lived with you from the 26th of July, 1910, till the morning of the 14th of September, 1911 ?'
Seddon: 'Yes.'
Attorney-General: 'Did you like her ?'
Seddon: 'Did I like her ?'
Attorney-General: 'Yes, that is the question.'

The second question threw Seddon off his balance because if he had said that he liked her it would have been difficult to explain why she had been buried in a pauper's grave, while if he had said that he did not like her it would have been hard to account for the fact that she had entrusted her money to him.

52. *R. v. Casement* [1917] 1 K.B. 98. The case involved the difficult legal question whether adherence to the King's enemies without the realm could constitute treason.

53. George S. Hellman's *Benjamin N. Cardozo* (1940), McGraw-Hill Book Company, Inc., is a valuable biography. *Selected Writings of Benjamin Nathan Cardozo* (1947), edited by Margaret Hall, with a foreword by Professor Patterson, Cardozo Professor of Jurisprudence, Columbia University School of Law, contains all his non-judicial writings. Many of his judgements have been collected in Dr. Beryl H. Levy's *Cardozo and Frontiers of Legal Thinking* (1938). In 1942 Chief Judge Irving Lehman delivered the first annual Cardozo lecture entitled *The Influence of Judge Cardozo on the Common Law* in which he analysed the work of his former colleague. No more eloquent tribute has ever been paid by one friend to another.

54. In the class vote Cardozo was voted the cleverest man and the second most modest.

55. John Purroy Mitchel was elected mayor of New York City in this election.

56. He became Chief Judge in 1927.

57. (1916) 217 N.Y. 382.

58. (1868) L.R. 3 H.L. 330.

59. [1932] A.C. 562.

60. (1922) 232 N.Y. 176.

61. [1935] 1 K.B. 146.

62. One of Cardozo's most interesting judgements was delivered in *Matter of Findlay* (1930) 253 N.Y. 1. A wife, having deserted her husband, went to live with her paramour and some years later had a son W. It was argued that W must be regarded as the legitimate son of the husband as he could have had access to his wife. Cardozo refused to apply the presumption of legitimacy to these facts, saying, 'There are breaths of human nature at which presumptions shrink and wither. . . . We have no thought to weaken the presumption of legitimacy by allowing its overthrow at the call of rumor or suspicion, or through inferences nicely poised. What we are now holding is in line with the historical development which has shorn the presumption of some of its follies and vagaries. . . . We have abandoned the ''nonsense'' of the rule of the four seas.'

63. *Selected Writings*, p. 178.

64. Ibid., p. 219.

65. Ibid., p. 254.

66. On 23 January 1932 the New York State Bar Association sent a telegram to President Hoover which concluded with these words: 'In the conviction that the matter is too important to be affected by geographical considerations and that only the welfare of the nation should be considered, this association presents the name of the man recognized by the profession and the people alike as the most distinguished jurist of our age—Chief Judge Benjamin N. Cardozo of the Court of Appeals of the State of New York.'

67. 305 U.S. p. xxviii.

68. Brandeis once said, 'Know book-keeping—the universal language of business', and later he added, 'My special field of knowledge is figures.'

69. *Selected Writings*, p. 105.

SUPPLEMENT
MR. JUSTICE FRANKFURTER
1882-1965

No other Justice of the United States Supreme Court has ever had so great an international reputation, especially in Great Britain, as did Felix Frankfurter who died in Washington on February 22nd. He was a distinguished judge, especially in the field of American constitutional law, an outstanding professor at the Harvard Law School, an able Government servant in various posts, and a most courageous man.

He was born in Vienna, on November 15, 1882, the descendant of five rabbis. His father, an unsuccessful business man, emigrated to the United States when F.F., as he was always known, was twelve. With his highly trained mind it was not difficult for him to learn English, which he sometimes used with the faint elaboration of an acquired skill, and to graduate seven years later from the College of the City of New York. He once said that, as part of his education, he assiduously read the *London Times* in the New York Public Library, both to improve his literary style and to study the British political system, which appealed to his imagination. In 1903 he entered the Harvard Law School from which he graduated three years later as head of his year and as an editor of the *Harvard Law Review*. The method of teaching, based on the " case system," a form of Socratic dialogue between the teacher and the students, was particularly suited to his quick, incisive mind. It was said that when, forty years later, he sat on the Supreme Court Bench, he sometimes employed this method when questioning counsel who was arguing a case before him, not always to the entire satisfaction of the latter.

After graduation he accepted an appointment as assistant to Henry L. Stimson who, at that time, was the United States Attorney for the Southern District of New York, occupied in large part in enforcing the Sherman Anti-Trust Act. Later in life Stimson, who was one of the greatest Americans of his generation, became Secretary of State under President Hoover, and Secretary of War, for the second time, under President Franklin D. Roosevelt. He was a decisive influence in F.F.'s life: this binding relationship between the reserved aristocrat from New England and the ebullient immigrant from New York was a tribute to both men. Their superficial differences proved no handicap because both of them were practical idealists with an intense devotion to work and service.

In 1911, when Stimson became Secretary of War under President Taft he took Frankfurter to Washington with him to be an officer in the Bureau of Insular Affairs. During the next three years F.F. shared a house, popularly known as " The House of Truth," with a number of brilliant young men, one of whom was Lord Eustace Percy, then attached to the British Embassy. Years later F.F. said that he represented for him all that was best in English life, and that he had helped to make him an Anglophile. It was also at this time that his life-long friendship with Mr. Justice Holmes began.

In 1914 he returned to the Harvard Law School as Byrne Professor of Administrative Law at the instance of Louis D. Brandeis, later to become Mr. Justice Brandeis, but in 1917 when the United States entered the First World War, he was again in Washington. He became assistant to the Secretaries of War and Labor and then chairman of the War Labor Policies Board. In 1918 he made to President Wilson his famous report on the Mooney-Billings case in which he concluded that Mooney had been unjustly convicted, but it took another twenty years before Mooney was pardoned.

In 1919 he returned to the Harvard Law School. Eight years later he issued another report on an even more famous murder trial. It took the form of an article in *The Atlantic Monthly* (March, 1927) entitled " The Portentous Case of Sacco and Vanzetti." He concluded that their trial before Judge Webster Thayer had been " a farrago of misquotations, misrepresentations, suppressions and mutilations." He faced with courage and dignity the wave of vilification that poured over him, including the effort made by some of Harvard's most distinguished alumni to have him removed from the Law School faculty. The unreasoning prejudice that blinded able and honest men and the unfortunate intervention of Professor John H. Wigmore, the leading authority on the law of evidence, led to the failure of all Frankfurter's efforts, but his work had permanent value. This has been eloquently stated by Dean Griswold [1]: " This debate had its own significance for the moment. But its great significance for others, I think, was the way it articulated Frankfurter's concern for the integrity of the judicial process. This is the great thing for which he has stood. This is the

[1] In 1962 the editors of the *Harvard Law Review* dedicated the November issue (76 Harv.L.Rev. 1–24) to Mr. Justice Frankfurter " on the occasion of his retirement from the Supreme Court and in honour of his eightieth birthday." The contributors were Mr. Justice John M. Harlan, Lord Evershed, Dean Erwin Griswold, Mr. Dean Acheson, Professor Paul A. Freund, Dr. Reinhold Niebuhr and Mr. Archibald MacLeish. The quotation from Dean Griswold is on p. 8.

great lesson that he has taught, to students of all ages, and for future generations as well as the present."

It also had significance for all law teachers. It taught them that they need not live in ivory towers, concerned only with law in the books. If they were to play their full part in the legal world they must instil in their students a realisation that they were members of a profession on which the welfare of the state depended, and that they had a public service to perform. It was for this reason that when the terrible Depression years descended on the country so many of F.F.'s ablest young men went to Washington to take part in the New Deal. He himself refused the office of Solicitor-General because he felt that his work at Harvard was more useful than any he could do at Washington. His enemies, of which there were not a few, described him as the " eminence grise " of the New Deal, but grey is hardly the colour one would ascribe to him. " Incandescent " would be a more accurate word.

In 1933–34 F.F. held the George Eastman Visiting Professorship at Oxford. In the book *Felix Frankfurter Reminisces* (1961) he described this year as " the fullest year my wife and I spent—the amplest and most civilised." It must be said that as a teacher he was only a limited success because the subjects he chose to deal with had little relevance for most of the English students, and the case method was an unaccustomed one for them. But in all other ways he played a leading, it might be said almost a dramatic, part. In a university which prides itself on its ability to converse, his conversations became famous. He dominated the talk, but he did not monopolise it. He was once described as a gay and cheerful Dr. Johnson, but unfortunately he did not have a Boswell to record his sayings. His professorship carried with it a fellowship at Balliol. He loved the College life, and was an assiduous and vocal attendant at all the meetings of the governing body. Dean Griswold [2] has said that at Harvard " Professor Frankfurter was not inarticulate in Faculty meetings. He was still the teacher, occasionally lecturing his colleagues. In this vein, he did not always effectively conceal a sense of his own rectitude. Occasionally there may even have been a detectable intimation that if his position was pure, that of those in opposition must be measurably impure." A similar intimation did not escape the notice of his Balliol colleagues, but they ascribed it to his being an American.

On January 5, 1939, President Roosevelt nominated F.F. to fill the vacancy created on the Supreme Court by the death of Justice Benjamin N. Cardozo. His nomination was bitterly opposed by

[2] *Op. cit.*, n. 1 at p. 10.

those who could not forget the part he had played in the *Sacco Vanzetti* case, but at the Senate committee hearing his replies were so dignified that he was confirmed by a voice vote of the Senate without objection. This was eminently fitting because no man was ever appointed to the Court who had a more profound knowledge of its history and procedure than he, as he had lectured and written on these subjects for nearly thirty years. On this experience he based the three fundamental principles which guided him throughout his judicial life.

The first principle concerned the primary importance of the fair trial, governed by proper rules of procedure. Here he was undoubtedly influenced by his memories of Mooney and Sacco and Vanzetti. The concept of the fair trial was, for him, the essence of the common law. He expressed this, perhaps most clearly, in his dissent in *Bridges* v. *California*, 314 U.S. 252 (1941). He rejected the view of the majority that " free speech and fair trials are two of the most cherished policies of our civilisation, and it would be a trying task to choose between them "; the majority conclusion was that " the substantive evil must be extremely serious and the degree of imminence extremely high before utterances can be punished." Frankfurter replied that " the majority do not in so many words hold that trial by newspapers has constitutional sanctity. But the atmosphere of their opinion and several of its phrases mean that or they mean nothing." There could, he insisted, be no due administration of justice if prejudice was uncontrolled. Perhaps his thesis has been best expressed in the recent report of the Warren Commission (p. 240): " Neither the press nor the public had the right to be contemporaneously informed by the police or prosecuting authorities of the details of the evidence being accumulated against Oswald. . . . The courtroom, not the newspaper or television screen, is the appropriate forum in our system for the trial of a man accused of a crime." These words must have seemed to Frankfurter to be an echo of the doctrine that he had advocated with passion for so many years.

The second principle that dominated Frankfurter's thoughts was that the Supreme Court in interpreting and applying the provisions of the Constitution must exercise the severest self-restraint. The provisions of Article V and of the Fourteenth Amendment that no person shall be deprived " of life, liberty, or property, without due process of law " could be interpreted so as to give the Supreme Court the power to invalidate any law which it regarded as unreasonable, and therefore, in its opinion, in conflict with due process of law. If this were accepted, then the " nine old men " in Washington would be the true " sovereign," as John Chipman Gray [3] once argued that they were, but this would be a denial of the democratic state.

How disastrous such a denial can be was conclusively illustrated by *Lochner* v. *New York*, 198 U.S. 45 (1905) in which the majority of the Supreme Court held a ten-hour law for bakers to be unconstitutional on the ground that it constituted an unreasonable limitation on freedom of contract. In his classic dissent Mr. Justice Holmes said: " The Fourteenth Amendment does not enact Mr. Herbert Spencer's Social Statics. . . . [A] constitution is not intended to embody a particular economic theory, whether of paternalism and the organic relation of the citizen to the State or of *laissez faire*." In his article "Mr. Justice Holmes and the Constitution" (1927–28, 41 Harv.L.R. 121, 144), Frankfurter summed up Holmes's philosophy: " Government means experimentation. To be sure, constitutional limitations confine the area of experiment. But these limitations are not self-defining and were intended to permit government. The door was left open to trial and error—' constitutional law like other mortal contrivances has to take some chances . . .' (*Blinn* v. *Nelson*, 222 U.S. 1, 7 (1911))."

Mr Justice Holmes fought, and finally won, the battle in so far as attempts were made by the Court to impose an economic doctrine on the national government or on the state legislatures. But Mr. Justice Frankfurter felt that this was only a partial victory because, as he saw it, the Court was now attempting to limit in other constitutional fields, especially those concerned with the so-called Bill of Rights of the first ten amendments, the power to experiment by the legislatures of the various states. This was being done by stating certain absolutes which were as rigid as the laws of the Medes and the Persians. Professor Freund [4] has summed up Frankfurter's reaction to this construction of the Constitution by referring to Lord Acton's counsel: " An absolute principle is as absurd as absolute power; and when you perceive a truth, look for the balancing truth." Frankfurter was always seeking for the balancing truth.

The third principle, which is closely akin to the second one, was stated by Frankfurter in his dissenting judgment in *Baker* v. *Carr*, 369 U.S. 186 (1962) known as the *Reapportionment Case*. He said: " The Court's authority—possessed of neither the purse nor the sword—ultimately rests on sustained public confidence in its moral sanction. Such feeling must be nourished by the Court's complete detachment, in fact and in appearance, from political entanglement

[3] *The Nature and Sources of the Law.*
[4] *Op. cit.*, n. 1 at p. 18.

and by abstention from injecting itself into the clash of political forces in political settlements." He concluded that " there is not under our Constitution a judicial remedy for every political mischief, for every undesirable exercise of legislative power." He therefore protested against placing on the courts " the task of accommodating the incommensurable factors of policy " when determining the relationship between population and legislative representation. Whether in the instant case the problem was as insoluble as Frankfurter thought it was is open to question, but that the Court should, wherever possible, avoid political entanglements is a rule of wisdom that cannot be too often repeated.

In the application of these three basic principles Frankfurter was following in the footsteps of his great predecessor, but he also did so in another equally important but less obvious way. For Holmes life was a series of experiments, but he also held that these could not be divorced from the past. " It ought always to be remembered that historic continuity with the past is not a duty; it is only a necessity." [5] This historic sense is an essential attribute of the legal scholar. It is not limited to book learning, for that may be arid : it refers to a method of thinking and a particular approach to legal problems considered as a part of " the seamless web " of the law. Mr. Justice Burton, in referring to Frankfurter, once spoke of " the importance of having a scholar on the court." This had been proved by Holmes whose classic work *The Common Law* is still regarded as compulsory reading in most of the law schools. It has been proved again by Frankfurter because he did not cease to be a scholar when he became a judge. He has been criticised for his many references to English legal history, but there is much to be said for his contention that the American Bill of Rights is related in more than name to the English one. He did not believe that a clear dividing line could be drawn at 1791 when the Amendments were ratified. He saw no conflict between the study of the past and of the present; he regarded them as complementary parts of a single whole.

Perhaps it was for this reason that he felt a special kinship with England and the English way of thinking. To say that he was an Anglophile, as has been done so often, is to sum up in a single, often misleading, word, a congeries of different ideas and beliefs. He loved the traditions and trappings of the past so that nothing gave him more pleasure than to wear the scarlet gown of Oxford, and he felt at home at the Bench of Gray's Inn as one the great company of common law judges who for more than seven hundred years had

[5] *Learning and Science. Occasional Speeches*, 84, 85.

administered " the law of the land." But perhaps most important
of all for him, was that here in England he found a society where
men were tolerant of each other's ideas, and could argue for hours
on end while still remaning friends. Dr. Reinhold Niebuhr,[6] writing
three years ago, summed up his passion for tolerance in these words:
" Frankfurter has been steadily governed, not by the principles of
liberalism or conservatism, but by his respect and veneration for the
long democratic tradition not only of this nation but of Great
Britain, in which tradition there was always an equal concern for
the security of the community on the one hand, and for the rights
of the individual on the other."

It was this desire to see both sides of a problem before reaching a
conclusion that made him both a great judge and a great man. It
may be said that in his love and respect for his fellow-men he
applied the ideals of the fair trial to life itself. But that his
judgments of men were also tempered by mercy did not surprise
those who understood him best.[7]

A. L. G.

---

[6] *Op. cit.*, n. 1 at p. 21.
[7] The last paragraph of Mr. Dean Acheson's tribute reads: " Over the years a
phrase keeps coming to my mind which seems to give the essence of my friend.
It is the title of a book which I read long ago, *The Loving Spirit.*" (*Op. cit.*,
n. 1, p. 16.)